Governance by Addiction

The Drug Addled Ideology of Modern Liberalism

By Martin R. Flowers

ISBN: 1500682632
ISBN-13: 978-1500682637

Martin R. Flowers

CONTENTS

Introduction

Many years ago, after graduating college and while working on my first book, *Null and Void,* I took a job as a "correctional advisor", which is a fancy way of saying corrections officer, in a suburb of Kansas City. Looking back on it now, it was a horrible job and I could not recommend anyone to work in that field. If I had it to do again, I would not have taken the job and found better things to do with my time. In the course of working in the corrections field, I was required to deal with drug addicts on a daily basis. The more time I spent around addicts the better I began to understand their thought process.

As the years have passed, I've found myself, like many U.S. citizens, frustrated by the direction our nation is headed. We seem to be on a slow downward spiral, lead by a government completely unwilling to accommodate the needs of its citizens. We've acted as spectators while one scandal after another plagues the far-left Obama

Administration. With each new scandal come an increasing number of lies, misdirection, and manipulations designed to confuse the public. To make matters worse, the media seems intent on continuing the lies for the benefit of those in power.

As each new scandal emerged, I began to see a familiar pattern. The liberal response to a problem always seemed to follow the same pattern I saw drug addicts use years before. I began looking at news stories involving liberal ideology and liberal websites. I was startled to see how often liberals engaged in this same pattern of behavior. The addict style behavior wasn't limited to responses to scandal; it was present in everything they did, from domestic policy to foreign policy.

The more I noticed the pattern the more interested I became in where the pattern began. How does a modern socio-political philosophy come to embrace the psychology of addiction? As I looked back on the early "progressive" thinkers liberals often embrace, I found a long list of individuals with histories of addiction. The fact is, liberal ideology did not come to embrace addiction over time, but actually grew out of addiction. Modern liberalism is the product of addiction.

The realization of liberalism's true origin became the genesis of this book. Once we understand the foundation upon which modern liberalism was built we can begin to minimize the ability of liberals to damage our nation. The goal of this book is to show the different ways addiction behavior manifests itself within the liberal ideology and how to develop policies which prevent these destructive behaviors from continuing unchecked.

Before going any further, I want to make a few issues clear. First, this is not a self help book. I am not an addiction medicine specialist and this book is not to be used to treat any medical condition. If you or a loved one has a problem with addiction, please seek professional medical help. Second, I am not saying all liberals are addicts. The ideas commonly referred to as modern liberalism sprang forth from the minds of individuals who were deep into serious addictions and as a result, their addicted minds influenced the ideas they developed. I would go one step further and say not all liberals are alike. My experience has shown me liberals exist in three forms. First is the common liberal voter. These are the individuals who are going along with the liberal ideology because they support some aspect of it. The individual may support the welfare state liberalism tends to create or they may support liberal views on other social issues. The common voting liberal generally mimics the actions of the other two forms.

The second group is the "thinkers". These are the liberals who often come up with wild ideas about how government should work and help to develop campaigns for liberal candidates. Most of this group is composed of college educated followers who are simply regurgitating what they were told by professors in college. I met a lot of these individuals while in college and their logic was flawed to anyone but themselves. These are the activists and protestors with the liberal movement. The "thinkers" are the public face of movements such as Occupy Wall Street, Earth Liberation Front, and other far left groups. These groups are looking to stir the pot and cause problem, never solve the problems.

The third group is the liberal "elite". These are the political and media leaders of the liberal movement. "Thinkers" who prove they are good workers in the activist causes become members of the "elite". Members of extremist liberal groups often find themselves working in high level positions within the government under a liberal administration. Liberal "elites" have spent enough time around the movement where they have come to understand the true goal is not to help humanity but to attain power.

These "elite" have begun to enact policies designed from the ground up to consolidate power into the hands of other "elites" within the liberal movement.

This book is about the "elite" of the liberal movement. While I will use the term "liberal" in this book, it is meant to describe the "elite" members only. While many of the concepts discussed in this book can be applied to the "voter" and "thinker" classes of the liberal movement, the full breadth of these tactics is only seen at the "elite" level.

Part I of this book will be a discussion of how the addiction behavior can be seen in liberal ideology. Part II, will be a discussion of how to curtail the destructive nature of the liberal ideology and help to revitalize the citizen's trust in government. The tool I propose for this is called the Government Accountability Pledge. The goal of this pledge will be to provide the accountability and transparency in government which the U.S. citizens deserve. Just as in my previous book, Part III is post script of how the concepts discussed in Part I and Part II applies within the lives of Christian believers today.

One final note before I finish this introduction. Every tactic I discuss in the following chapters will be used by liberals to attack this book, myself and the conservative movement. Every time liberals use these tactics it will serve as validation of the theory presented in these pages.

Chapter 1: In the Beginning There Was...Opium

There are many different sources one can cite for the foundation of modern liberalism. However, one of the most often cited is the economic theories of Karl Marx. Throughout the mid 19th Century, Marx wrote extensively about the issues of class struggle, economic equality and workers rights. These writings have become some of the most read political texts in the world, and their virtues are trumpeted by liberals everywhere. However, as George Fabian discusses in his comprehensive Marx biography, "Karl Marx - Prince of Darkness", Marx was an opium addict[1]. With this knowledge in hand it should come as no surprise then that Marx's ideas were flawed. Marxism and Communism both fail to work because they're not based in reality but in a drug addled fictional world created within Marx's mind.

Nowhere in Marx's writings are the effects of drugs more evident than in his comments on class struggle. In Marx's drug induced state he sees everything as "black and white". The class struggle is between the Bourgeoisie and the Proletariat, the rich and the poor, the upper class and the lower working class. Marx, along with many of his contemporaries, believed the working class would eventually rise up to overthrow the upper class. However, Marx's vision of a revolution and successful socialist utopia were nothing more than a figment of his opium controlled imagination. In reality, Marx's own upper-middle class upbringing proved his theory wrong[2].

Unfortunately, these drug induced ideas have continued on in our society. To this day we're forced to deal with the political left's attempts to destroy the middle class in some vain attempt to fulfill Marx's dream. Marx's dream of a worker's revolt cannot occur as long as the middle class exists to bridge the socio-economic gap between the two classes. The reality of society being better off with a middle class of educated citizens who propel the economy forward is actually seen as bad within liberal ideology.

Marx's ideas made their way to the United States in the later half of the 19th century. German immigrants brought this new liberal ideology to the U.S. While Marx did write for

American newspapers, those writings generally were limited to articles related to current events. Liberals saw the United States as the prefect storm for the rise of their workers revolt. The United States presented a democratically elected government where the public was preconditioned to believe the workers should have a say in how things were done. Convincing the common U.S. citizen to accept the ideas of Karl Marx wasn't difficult, particularly with limited literacy among many working class citizens. This isn't to say U.S. citizens would accept Marx's ideas in a broad brush stoke, but rather they began to accept the ideas in small amounts when woven into the preexisting fabric of American politics.

In the decades following Marx, the world saw the rise of another philosopher who greatly influenced modern liberalism. Friedrich Nietzsche has become a well known German philosopher, having written a number of books in the 1880s. The central theme of Nietzsche's works is the "will to power", the notion that humanity is driven to power over all other goals[3]. This is an idea which finds particular meaning with the liberal "elite". The liberal drive for power over other humans is found in Nietzsche's writings as it seems the natural course of humanity, for certain people to have power over others.

Nietzsche also became famous for his 1883 book *Thus Spoke Zarathustra* in which he proclaimed "God is dead"[4]. In his books, Nietzsche was well known for his disparaging tone towards Christianity and any belief in God. It became so bad that he could not find a job as a college professor due, in large part, to these beliefs. In an 1883 letter to his former student Peter Gast, Nietzsche complained of wanting revenge against those who opposed his ideas and caused him to be denied employment[5]. The resentment Nietzsche shows in his letters is very typical of what we see in liberals today when conservatives challenge their beliefs.

It should come as no surprise to see these feelings in Nietzsche's writings. Many scholars acknowledge that by the 1880s Nietzsche was using massive quantities of opium. In the 2005 biography, *Friedrich Nietzsche*, scholar Curtis Cates notes that Nietzsche had even taking to writing his own fraudulent prescriptions in 1883 to obtain drugs[6]. It was in this drug addled state that Nietzsche wrote of the death of God and the drive for humans to attain power over the rest of humanity. These very ideas have become the building blocks of modern liberal ideology and continue to form the policies of our nation, which I will describe later in this book.

If Marx was the match and Nietzsche was the wood stoking the destructive fire of modern liberal ideology, then Sigmund Freud was the can of gasoline which turned it into a raging inferno. Liberals love Sigmund Freud. It was Freud who gave us the modern techniques of psychoanalysis, and if you're a liberal "elite" looking to control people what better place to start than by learning how people think. One of Freud's best known contributions to the field of psychology is the division of the psyche known as the Id, the Ego and the Super Ego[7]. The reason this is so important to liberals is the Id is seen as the more child like impulsive portion of the psyche. According to Freud's theory, the driving force behind the Id is what he referred to as the "pleasure principle". Where Nietzsche believed it was power which provided the driving force behind human actions, Freud believed it was the desire to attain pleasure and avoid pain[8].

The aspect of society where we see liberals utilize the pleasure principle the most is in the liberal dominated entertainment industry. Liberals within the entertainment industry look for ways to utilize Freud's idea of a pleasure driven mind. It's actually a very simple concept, by appealing to their desire for pleasure; most people don't even realize they're losing their rights. Think of how destructive this is, by connecting pleasure to abandoning their rights, individuals are convinced that losing right is a good thing. Imagine a television show which creates pleasure and feeds the Id, but also portrays guns as being bad. The connection made in the unconscious mind is that seeing guns as bad makes a person feel good, so banning guns will also make the person feel good. Understanding of the Id is the driving force behind liberal uses of shame, intimidation and guilt to convince individuals to follow destructive ideas.

Like Marx and Nietzsche before him, Freud also attacked Christianity and religion in general. Freud held that God was an imaginary being devised by humans to deal with problems in life and society[9]. The ideas Freud developed about God and religion were the next ideological step to help further the ideas liberals pursue today. Freud took his disbelief in God further than Marx and Nietzsche by arguing that religion and the idea of an all powerful deity were nothing more than a creation of the mind, developed for the purpose of conquering the fears people have of the unknown world around them. These ideas, developed by Freud, are still in use by mental health professionals today as seen in the manuals used to diagnose mental disorders. According to these manuals, religious belief is a mental disorder.

It should come as no surprise to discover Freud was also like Marx and Nietzsche in being a drug addict. Freud not only used cocaine, but wrote multiple academic papers supporting the use of cocaine[10]. After witnessing the devastating effects of cocaine on patients, Freud appears to have stopped writing about medical uses of cocaine. However, according to his letters he was still take the substance himself[11]. In fact there is virtually no hard evidence to prove Freud ever stopped taking cocaine. The very fact that Freud claims to be using cocaine to treat his own depression would seem to indicate his continuing addiction since depression is a symptom of cocaine withdrawal.

Once again, in Freud we see a prominent figure in the liberal ideology who was a drug addict. Freud, Marx and Nietzsche are seen as the leaders in the liberal pantheon. This is not to say there were no other philosophers who have influenced the modern liberalism. However, these three men created the concepts of wealth redistribution, the deified state and the pleasure driven mind, which form the foundation of modern liberal ideology. As a result, it comes as little surprise to see liberals rewrite the histories of these and other noted liberals of the past. While it's know that drug use and addiction were problems for these individuals, very little is written about it and most of the evidence is the result of letters they left behind. The liberal desire to recreate Freud, Marx and Nietzsche, among others, is not limited to minimizing the effects of drug use on their ideologies. In recent years, liberal scholars have begun to push the idea of all three of these men being homosexual. The goal appears to be to recreate these men in the ideal liberal image and hide the flaws which undercut the liberal ideology.

The drug use and revisionist tendencies of the liberal movement continue through the 1960s until this very day. I could write an entire book about the elite liberals who did drugs during the 1960s while developing the ideas they use today to destroy our nation. As time went on, the drugs which are used have become more exotic and the damage done by the liberal ideology has grown more destructive. We need look no further than the nightly news to see evidence of the damage liberalism is causing. The states with the most liberal governments and policies are the states legalizing drugs such as marijuana, while at the same time imposing draconian laws on gun ownership and religious freedoms.

In the coming chapters of Section One we will look at the different ways the modern liberal movement continues to display behavior commonly associated with drug addiction. The goal is to recognize this behavior so it can be curtailed before more damage is done to the U.S. citizens.

Study Questions:

1: Can you think of when these drug addled ideas harmed you?
2: How did you feel to be victimized by these liberal ideas?
3: What was the goal the liberal movement was trying to achieve?
4: Did they achieve their goal?
5: Do the ideas developed by men like Freud lead to a greater level of control?
6: What can be done to prevent these ideas from being used against the public?

Chapter 2: Lies and Misleading

Everyone lies; let's just get that out of the way. Lying in and of itself is not special to addiction. However, in working around addicts I learned there is a subtle difference in the reason for the lies. Most people lie to get out of a problem or stay out of a problem, normally one we created for ourselves. The classic example of this would be the husband who tells his wife she looks good in a pair of jeans when she doesn't. While I don't condone the husband lying to his wife, I do understand his desire to keep her happy and avoid a conflict. Addicts are different in that the lies they tell are often related to the justification of their behaviors as related to their addiction. I've lost track of how many times while working in the corrections field I was told by offenders there was an underlying medical condition that required them to be a drug addict. I don't know how many times I've read police reports where an addict stole something and then insisted they had the owners' permission to take it. I couldn't even begin to count how many times I've heard of alcoholics who insist they only drank one beer and their metabolism is just messed up and it causes them to appear drunk when they really are not.

Liberals engage in this same type of lying to justify behavior. I could cite a multitude of examples of this behavior, but I want to focus on two examples. The first is the 2014 trade of five Taliban prisoners for a U.S. POW held by the Taliban. We heard every lie imaginable regarding this situation, from Sgt. Bowe Bergdahl being in danger[1], to it making the transition for the Afghanistan government easier[2], and even the Obama administration, seemingly, claiming the President signed off on the deal[3]. As each lie was exposed, a new lie was developed to cover the pervious lie. When the criticism of the prisoner exchange began to grow, the lies seemed to grow along side. It got to the point where the White House claimed it was not possible to tell Congress about the deal for Bergdahl's release[4]. Claims of soldiers being placed in more danger due to the trade were met with cynical responses. The Secretary of State referred to such criticism as "baloney" despite the clear evidence to the contrary[5].

The second example is the "Operation Fast and Furious" scandal. Despite mountains of evidence suggesting this was a botched operation which should have never been undertaken in the first place, the Obama administration continued to insist there was no wrong doing. To make matters worse, instead of taking responsibility for the deaths which occurred due to the weapons being transferred to known criminals, the liberals used those deaths as fuel for their attacks on the Second Amendment. Attempts by members of Congress to uncover the truth were met with obstruction and more lies[6]. At no point has the Obama administration offered any reasonable explanation for what occurred during "Operation Fast and Furious". It seems there is a larger problem with federal government operations in the Phoenix area regarding the Veteran's Administration. If the Obama administration had been forthright about "Operation Fast and Furious", would we have learned about the problems at the Phoenix Veteran's Administration facility sooner and saved some lives?

In both of these cases, the liberals have continued to lie about the issues in order to justify what they know are policy decisions detrimental to the well being of our nation. However, lying is not the only avenue liberals have at their disposal. In many cases, a simple attempt to mislead the public is sufficient without the need for bold faced lies. Examples of this can be seen in the economic numbers the government generates. The Obama administration has been notorious for cherry picking job growth numbers to make the economy look much better than it really is. We would regularly see news reports of job growth when in reality there was a net loss of employment. The favorite tactic for misleading the public about the economy seems to be the number of unemployment claims. As time goes by, the number of people who are long term unemployed and claiming unemployment benefits will go down. People who fall off the unemployment rolls as a result of attrition are not the same as people finding gainful employment.

Another area where liberals use misleading to impose their political will is in regards to environmental policies. Despite what some conservatives want you to believe, environmental policies are good for the public and business. Reducing the amount of trash we send to landfills lowers taxes and helps to promote better land use options. Reducing wasteful usage of water means your local government has to buy less of the chemicals needed to treat water. In short, environmental sustainability is one of the few win-win scenarios in public policy when developed and applied appropriately. Unfortunately, modern liberalism despises win-win scenarios. As a result, we see bad policy such as cap and trade which imposes significant financial burdens on both the individual and the business community. Liberals argue the cost being incurred by cap and trade is a good trade off because of the reduction in carbon emissions. The problem is, it's impossible to statistically prove there is a corresponding reduction due to cap and trade. The amount of carbon in the earth's atmosphere is a tiny fraction of a percent[7]. To make matters worse, the government fails to provide the standard error for the sample size. As a result, we can't prove if a policy like cap and trade is having any impact, be it positive or negative.

One of the favorite policy areas where liberals use misleading information is gun control. Listening to misleading liberal rhetoric, we are lead to believe gun violence is at a record high and the only means of stopping the senseless killings is to ban all firearms. Statistics from the FBI prove beyond any doubt that gun violence in the United States is on a sharp downturn and has been falling each year since states began adopting conceal carry laws[8]. Despite these facts liberals continue to insist gun violence is on the increase and use this misleading information to convince the public to adopt more gun control laws. Of course, when the facts prove liberals wrong then they start misleading the public by confusing established words. The far left has taken to using misleading words to describe various firearms. For example, according to liberals the AR in AR-15 stands for assault rifle. When in actuality, the AR in AR-15 stands for Armalite Rifle, named after the company where it was first created. Secondly, an assault rifle is a select fire weapon system used by the military and is currently stringently regulated as a Class III firearm under the National Firearms Act, a category into which the AR-15 does not fit. Neither of these facts has stopped liberals from their endless attempts to ban this extremely versatile firearm from being owned by the American public.

For liberals the use of lies and misleading terminology is simply a means to the end goal. As long as they increase their control and bring us closer to their ultimate goal nothing else matters. This is similar to a drug addict. The primary goal of the addict is to get their next high. Their desire for the high, driven by their chemical dependence, is so strong that they will disregard reality and pursue their goal no matter the consequences. Liberals are addicted to controlling others and as a result they will lie and mislead the public to gain that control. The result, whether it's releasing known terrorists, giving firearms to criminals or developing disastrous economic policies, is justified as long as they gain more control over the public.

Study Questions:

1: Can you think of a time where you saw liberals lying or misleading the public?
2: How did you feel about the lies they were telling?
3: What was the goal of the lies and misleading statements?
4: Did they achieve their goal?
5: Did the tactics lead to a greater level of control?
6: What could have been done to prevent the lying and misleading?

Chapter 3: Manipulation and Controlling Others

Manipulation and controlling are common among addicts, based on my experience. I cannot begin to count how many disciplinary reports I wrote as a corrections officer because of offenders with addiction issues who tried to manipulate staff. My personal observation was that most times the addict was trying to manipulate the staff into engaging in enabling activity. The far left has been using manipulation for years to pursue their liberal agenda. In many cases, this type of manipulation has been rather transparent such as the left leaning media reporting stories with a liberal slant. These types of press manipulation are nothing new, and began with concepts such as "yellow journalism" and "vox populi" in the late 19th Century.

However, there are two more recent types of manipulation the liberals' ideology promotes which are much more concerning to the continuity of our form of government. The first is historical revision. Up until recently, it was difficult to revise history to meet a particular political leaning. Doing so required the destruction and reprinting of books which supported the regimes ideology. When history has been rewritten in the past, it was typically done by totalitarian regimes and it was very apparent when it happened. After all, huge bonfires of burning books generally don't go unnoticed by the rest of the world.

Recently, we have seen a change in the way manipulation occurs due, in large part, to advances in technology. Today, there is no need to burn books when the same purpose can be accomplished by rewriting some computer code for a website. More and more we are seeing websites being edited by government agencies with the intention of manipulating how the public views policy. It's becoming commonplace for the government to delete material off the internet and even ask search and service providers to block these searches. In some cases, the Obama Administration has gone so far as to have documents removed from internet archive sites to prevent further dissemination[1]. A government seeking to prevent the public from learning the truth is a government the public cannot trust. Governments generally hide information from the public when the government officials know the activity they're engaged in is either illegal action or would be found objectionable by the public. The only reason we know the Obama Administration has been conducting this type of activity is because of internet activists and alternative media journalists who had found these documents and saved them before the documents were removed.

Another way the far left uses manipulation to sway public opinion is what's known as "fifth column politics". The way this type of manipulation works is by creating a false appearance of their political enemies. This is often times accomplished by sending liberal operatives into a situation to act as conservatives and cause a public scene. Liberal operatives often times take on the appearance of conservative groups and use similar language, but it's often over the top in rhetoric and appearance. The goal is to make conservatives look incompetent, hateful or in some other way unappealing to the voting public. The most common form of this tactic is known as the "agent provocateur", were someone is sent into a protest event with the intention of making the protesters look bad.

There are some cases where fifth column politics takes on a much more complex appearance. Having lived in Kansas my entire life I have grown accustom to the unwanted sight of protesters from Westboro Baptist Church. While many are somewhat familiar with the now deceased founder of the church, Fred Phelps, many are not aware of his long history with liberal causes and the Democratic Party. I'm not going to spend a lot of time covering the history in depth. For those interested, there are a number of good articles online which cover this issue[2]. Up until the mid 1980s, Phelps was a golden boy of the Kansas Democratic Party, having won nomination for state office on multiple occasions. Then something happened and former civil rights attorney Fred Phelps became the epitome of a supposedly hateful and backwards conservative Christian element of the GOP. However, even after this transformation, Phelps and his "church" continued close ties with the Democratic Party and other liberal causes.

When confronted with this information liberal's claim Phelps was a "blue dog Democrat" who never changed party allegiance. However, in looking at the political activities of the Phelps family it's clear how wrong the liberal claim is. The example of Westboro Baptist Church is simply the height of liberal manipulation. This particular manipulation has been so successful because it has been multi-faceted. First, it helped the far left attack the "religious right" segment of the Republican Party in the late 1980s. Secondly, it has helped to force down membership in evangelical Christian congregations across the U.S. with the result of leaving citizens feeling more hopeless and in need of the government. Third, it has provided a rallying point for the homosexual community. This third facet of the manipulation shows the true nature of modern liberalism. There is simply no place for homosexuals within the adapted socialist ideology of modern liberalism. Anyone who questions this fact needs to look no further than the last century of world history to see how socialist governments have treated homosexuals for proof. The liberal manipulation of the homosexual community has been so complete that they are being lead like lambs to the slaughter and don't realize it.

Manipulation almost always leads to some form of control. Based on my observations, drug addicts tend to exert control over others in very subtle ways. It tends to be something as simple as getting money for their next fix or getting someone to help them acquire an item they want. In some cases, the goal is to get someone to help them either avoid or reduce the effect of the consequences of their addiction. This is where enabling is so harmful to the addict, because only after they have been forced to deal with the full consequences of their addiction will they actually seek help for it.

Modern liberalism utilizes this same mechanism of control but in a much different way. Liberalism seeks to control people in order to maintain political power. The best example of this can be seen in the liberal attempts to enact gun control. The liberal media argues for increased gun control because of deaths associated with gun violence. . However, they fail to mention the statistics which show a decrease in violent crime over the last decade as concealed carry laws have become more common[3]. The liberal media also fails to mention that many firearm related deaths are the result of law enforcement using firearms to protect the public and accidental shootings.

The true goal of gun control legislation is not to control firearms but to enable the far left to strengthen their control over the government and by extension, the public. I'm not going to begin a diatribe on why gun control is bad. If you want to read that, feel free to go online and look at the proverbial metric ton of ink which has been spilt on the issue. My intention here is not to discuss the pros and cons of gun control but to discuss why liberals want gun control as a means of controlling the public. Some of this is a repeat of ideas I wrote about in my first book, *Null and Void,* so I apologize in advance for those who have read this before. However, I'm sure a refresher course on this issue will not hurt you.

Despite what liberals want us to believe, the U.S. Constitution is not a "living document". The Constitution is a historical document that must be interpreted based on its historical context. There is no place where this is more apparent than in the Bill of Rights. In their wisdom, our nation's founders looked to establish legal protections to ensure the tools required to attain freedom from British rule were present for future generations. The amendments enumerated in the Bill of Rights form the backbone of our government, providing the citizens with the means of ensuring continuity of representation.

The Second Amendment is the final check and balance in our system of government. When a liberal talks about repealing or in any other way limiting the power of the Second Amendment, they are in essence saying they want to do away with our form of government. Would we, willingly, accept a President who would dissolve the Supreme Court or permanently disband Congress? Absolutely not! However, as we have seen time and again throughout Obama's imperial presidency, nothing seems to stand in the way of strengthening the liberal's grip on power. Once the citizens lose the ability to fight back, the liberals can execute whatever form of control they desire.

Clearly, one of the primary goals of the liberal ideology is control. The liberal hatred of individuality is one of the driving forces behind their desire to control the public. We see this aspect of control throughout the liberal ideology, from gun control to education. The new Common Core standards are an excellent example of how liberalism looks to destroy individuality. Whether the education is right or wrong doesn't matter as long as everyone is taught exactly the same and the end result is conformity. Functional societies simply cannot exist when the public is subject to extreme repression and control. Unfortunately, the creation of a dysfunctional society by undermining the right of individuals helps further the goal of control by establishing a situation where more governmental control is required.

Study Questions

1: Can you think of a time where you saw liberals manipulating the public?
2: How did you feel about the manipulation?
3: What was the goal of the manipulation?
4: Did they achieve their goal?
5: Did the manipulation lead to a greater level of control?
6: What could have been done to prevent the manipulation?

Chapter 4: Confusing the Issue and the Blame Game

During my time around drug addicts, I discovered they never wanted to acknowledge they had a problem until they hit rock bottom. This isn't any new insight on addicted behavior, just confirmation of what we already know. What amazed me was the extent addicts will go to in order to avoid accepting their addiction and the need for help. Often times they would try confusing the issue, claiming their addiction really wasn't a problem. In fact, they would claim the only reason they were in a correctional facility is because the law had a problem with drugs. Inevitably, they would about talk how much money could be made legalizing various drugs and all the supposed good they believe can come from drug use. All of this was meant to take your mind off the issue of them breaking the law.

Liberals have become experts at confusing issues. The purpose of the liberal media is to muddy the waters of truth so much so as to prevent the public from knowing what is really going on in the world around them. Confusing the issue is also a common tactic used by liberals to attack whistleblowers. When someone reports government wrongdoing the liberal response is to dig up dirt on the person and attack them. This is what's referred to as an ad hominem fallacy. The goal is to distract you from the real issue by attacking the individual who identified the problem. When I worked in corrections, offenders would do this all the time. They would claim my coworkers were saying things about me or that another offender threatened them.

One of the places where we see this with liberals is regarding health care reform. In the build up to the passing of the Affordable Care Act, (a.k.a. Obamacare) we heard liberals talk about how the primary issue needed for reform was to provide access to care and this could only be accomplished by requiring everyone to buy insurance. The fact of the matter is, access to care was never really the issue. Prior to the enactment of the Affordable Care Act, faith based hospitals were providing billions of dollars in free medical care across this nation each year[1]. I personally saw inmates receive free medical treatment at faith based hospitals. In reality, there was no problem with access to care, only a problem with individuals not knowing how to get access.

The idea of access to care and mandated insurance coverage was nothing more than an attempt by liberals to confuse the real issues which needed to be addressed in any real health care reform. The issues, which actually needed to be addressed included: making healthy living a goal of our nation, ending a for-profit health care system and finding ways to increase the economic opportunities for individuals, thus allowing them better access to care. These are all ideas I covered in my first book, *Null and Void.* One of the main problems our health care system is facing is the enormous strain being placed on it. Where reforms in the areas I mentioned would help to reduce the strain, liberals are looking to increase the strain by pushing more and more people into the system. Where conservative goals would require health insurance companies to pay for fitness club memberships, the liberals want to force health insurance companies to pay for elective gender reassignment surgery[2].

Liberals wish to confuse the issue because they don't want the public to know there are other options. The last thing liberals want the public to know is there are not just other options, but better options which could serve to help individuals achieve the American Dream. Modern liberalism is all about control, and by confusing the issues and diverting attention from real solutions which could better our society. Instead of embracing real solutions to problems, liberals create more problems in their vain attempts to gain more control over individuals.

Earlier I wrote about faith based hospitals providing free care to millions of people each year. Unfortunately, many of the health insurance policies sold through the federal exchange do not provide coverage for treatment at these same hospitals. For liberals to leave faith based hospitals out in the cold in these policies should not come as a surprise. These same faith based hospitals have elected to stand by their faith, and in doing so have infuriated the far left by refusing to perform abortions. In looking at abortion, we see yet another example of how liberals confuse an issue to distract the public from recognizing their bad policies.

The very notion of referring to the supporters of abortion as "pro-choice" is laughable. I wrote about this in my first book, but it bears repeating here. If two consenting adults make the choice to have sexual relations, and two consenting adults make the choice not to use the appropriate protection, then those two consenting adults made the choice to have a child. For someone to then argue for the right to make a choice after making a series of bad choices is ridicules. There are few, if any, "do-overs" in life. When an individual makes a choice they need to live with the consequences of the choice they made. The issue of abortion highlights exactly how liberalism derives its thought process from drug addiction by confusing the issue, making the murder of an unborn child seem like it's a matter of free choice, responsibility and individuality when nothing could be further from the truth. Abortion, as a means of birth control, is nothing more than a selfish act designed to deprive an unborn child of free choice and individuality.

When confusing the issues doesn't work, drug addicts will often resort to the blame game. If I had a penny for every time an addict told me" it was someone else's fault", I would be a very rich man. It was not uncommon, when doing room searches, for me to find a piece of contraband in an offender's locker. Upon being confronted, they would accuse someone else of putting it there. Police officers deal with this all the time, they find some illegal drugs in a car with multiple occupants and everyone wants to blame someone else for the drugs. The goal of the blame game is to deflect attention from the guilty party.

We've seen liberals play the blame game time and again. In fact, during his first term in office, President Obama made an art of blaming former President George W. Bush anytime something went wrong. President Obama blamed Bush so often it's become a running joke. If you had asked President Obama how many people it took to change a light bulb in the White House, he would say he didn't know, but it must have been Bush's fault that the light bulb burned out.

The epitome of the blame game occurred towards the end of President Obama's first term when militants associated with Al Qaida attacked a U.S. diplomatic post in Benghazi, Libya on September 11th, 2012. The attack left three U.S. citizens dead and a lot of unanswered questions. Unfortunately, the Obama Administration and their liberal friends were more concerned with placing blame elsewhere than with accepting responsibility for what happened. In the immediate aftermath of the attack, the Obama administration placed the blame on an internet video which was seen as disparaging to the Islamic faith[3]. The federal government went so far as to arrest the video's producer for violating his conditions of release for a previous criminal conviction[4]. Coincidently, the previous conviction had nothing to do with making internet videos or insulting Islam. To this day, we have yet to get straight answers about Benghazi from the Obama Administration, and just like with Operation Fast and Furious, we continue to see obstruction and the blaming others as the standard liberal operating procedure to delay any investigation.

The tactics of confusing the issue and blaming others have been pretty common for both liberals and drug addicts for a long time. Going all the way back to Karl Marx, these tactics have served to deceive the public into following policies which are detrimental to the well being of our nation. From confusing the issues of health care and abortion to blaming an internet video for three U.S. citizens who died heroically serving their country, modern liberalism has made a science of confusing the U.S. citizens for their own political gain.

Study Questions:

1: Can you think of a time where you saw liberals trying to confuse an issue or blame someone?
2: How did you feel about the tactic?
3: What was the goal of the confusion or blame the liberals were trying to create?
4: Did they achieve their goal?
5: Did the tactics lead to a greater level of control?
6: What could have been done to prevent the confusion or blaming from occurring?

Chapter 5:
Divide and Conquer

Addicts always seem to look for ways to drive a wedge between people. If you've ever been friends with an addict then you've probably experienced the destructive effect they have on your other relationships. I saw the same effect play out among offenders. Whenever they were getting into trouble for something they would begin to tell me about all the horrible things my co-workers were supposedly saying about me. The truth is the tactic of divide and conquer is as old as the modern liberal ideology itself, tracing its roots back to Marx. The whole idea behind Marx concept of class struggle was to provoke a conflict between the rich and the poor. Marx intended to use the poor as a fighting force to overthrow the rich and in the power vacuum which followed, he and his drug addled friends would impose their own sense of justice and government. The world watched in horror as this plan played out in Russia in 1917, Germany in both 1918 and in 1933, and China in 1949. In all of these cases, a large segment of the population was convinced they had "nothing to lose but their chains[1]" and attacked the intellectual and elite of their society. The end result was societies which failed to function, economies which grew stagnant and mass graves full of anyone who disagreed with the leftist ideology.

This same tactic of divide and conquer is playing out in our society today. The liberal elite here in the United States are well aware of the plan and what they need to do to bring it to fruition. One of the primary goals which must be accomplished is the destruction of the middle class. The middle class functions as a bridge connecting the wealthy and the impoverished and acts as a gateway to a better life. Modern liberals are infuriated by the notion of the middle class providing an avenue for individuals to create a better life. According to the liberal ideology, the only means of achieving a better life must be through a progressive government. This simply goes to show the liberal ideologies is about controlling others. The liberal ideology is born out of drug addiction and the resulting lack of self control. Because of this lack of self control, liberalism looks to exert control on others to compensate as discussed in Chapter 3.

However, when liberals find they can't control a certain aspect of society, they seek to destroy it as we see happening with the middle class. As must of us know by now, the favorite tool the liberal has for attacking the middle class is taxes. I remember during the early years of President Clinton's first term he introduced a package of social programs and famously said "I will not raise taxes on the middle class to pay for these programs"[2]. After saying this, President Clinton and his cronies in Congress hit the middle class with one of the largest tax increase in U.S. history[3]. While the lie was troubling, the chilling effect it had on the middle class was more disturbing. During the early years of the Obama Administration we saw similar actions designed to cut the middle class of any spending power. The new taxes established by the Affordable Care Act, in combination with the increased cost of health insurance, have left many middle class families struggling.

When taxing the middle class into extinction isn't enough, the liberals attack the small businesses which form the backbone of the middle class. Heavy handed regulations on everything from health care, to labor issues and environmental laws have prevented many small businesses from expanding[4]. It is becoming increasingly unprofitable for small businesses to operate in many parts of the United States. Let there be no doubt, the liberals are doing this on purpose. By slowing the growth of small businesses the liberals effectively force more citizens below the poverty level and thus onto government subsidies. As more small businesses fail under the increasing burden of federal regulation, the number of unemployed and underemployed will continue to grow. From the liberal point of view, the more people who are living below the poverty level, the more people they have available to take part in their Marx inspired worker's revolt. The goal is to drive as many people as possible below the poverty level to increase the labor force for their own plans.

In some cases, liberals have found creative ways to attack the middle class. During the mid 1990's, liberals forced legislation through Congress to require lending institutions to provide home loans to at risk parties[5]. Liberals trumpeted the change as a means of giving the American Dream to people who needed a hand up. Unfortunately, nothing could have been further from the truth. These changes often resulted in lenders making home loans to borrowers who lacked the financial ability to pay their bills. The combination of bad loans and adjustable interest rate mortgages left many homeowners drowning in debt with no escape. Finally, the tidal wave of this disaster came crashing down in 2008 when the market tumbled and lenders began to fail. The liberal elite didn't feel the impact of the economic disaster they created because they knew not to invest in the market during that time. Furthermore, the high risk borrowers had nothing to lose to begin with, since they had nothing when they started and they had nothing in the end. The group who really lost was the middle class who saw their retirement funds devastated practically overnight. Many older workers who were expecting to retire in comfort quickly found their retirement fund nearly gone. Now many of those retirees are living below the poverty level and relying increasingly on government programs for their survival. As a result, government programs are under more stress and have long waiting lists, a perfect example is the situation with the Veterans Administration.

Recently, we've seen the same tactic used to create the housing bubble being repackaged to attack the middle class in a different way. Realizing the resilient nature of the middle class, liberals have elected to force the middle class into poverty through massive hikes in the minimum wage. There have been protests nationwide calling for a $15 per hour minimum wage and the City of Seattle has already approved a local ordinance requiring a $15 an hour minimum wage[6]. The result of these minimum wage hikes will be three fold. First, it will cause an exponential increase in inflation to keep up with the influx of money into the economy, with the resulting rise in the cost of everyday items people need to survive. Secondly, it will hasten the failure of many small businesses due to their being unable to pay the increased wages. While people will have more money, it will not go as far due to steep inflation. As a result, consumers will be spending less money on nonessential items and will be flocking to discount stores for essential items in the hope of stretching their paycheck. The third impact will be the snowball effect all of this will have on the government. As more people lose their jobs and the cost of living increases, the government will be under a greater burden to provide subsidies for individuals living below the poverty level. As a result the government will be forced to raise taxes, thus causing more businesses to shutter their doors. Left unchecked the cycle would continue until we reach a breaking point where the government is unable to squeeze any more tax dollars out of the economy and the liberals finally have their much dreamed of workers revolt.

Liberals are determined to create their much beloved workers revolt anyway they can. There is no concern for who gets hurt or any other consequences as long as the middle class is destroyed and the revolt takes place. Furthermore, the liberals concern for the needs of the working class is phony. This is why we see liberals appearing in the media talking about being broke when in reality they are multimillionaires. The goal of liberal ideology is to create a socialist utopia with the liberal elite in charge and the working class is nothing more than cannon fodder for the liberal cause.

Study Questions:

1: Can you think of a time where you saw liberals using the tactic of divide and conquer?
2: How did you feel about the tactic?
3: What was the goal of the division the liberals were trying to create?
4: Did they achieve their goal?
5: Did the tactics lead to a greater level of control?
6: What could have been done to prevent the divide and conquer tactic from being used?

Chapter 6:
Paranoia and Denial

Stories about the paranoia of drug addicts are common. It seems someone is always out to get them. While working in corrections, I came across an offender who epitomized this aspect of addiction. This particular offender had just finished serving a punishment for a rule infraction at the facility. I tried to enter into a conversation with the offender to ask what he had learned from breaking the rule and the ensuing punishment. The offender wasn't interested in talking about what happened. He was obsessed with the supervisor who caught him breaking the rule. The offender insisted the supervisor was out to get him and no matter what I said I couldn't change his mind. There is something about drug use which seems to cause paranoid thoughts. I don't know if it's a chemical reaction in the brain caused by the drug use or a habit created by doing something illegal and constantly worrying if they're going to be caught. Whichever it is, paranoia is clearly part of addiction.

As with addiction, paranoia seems to be a key component in the liberal ideology. Paranoia with liberals also mimics addiction in that it takes on many different forms, from the basic to the more outlandish. It's become almost cliché for liberals to claim there is a "vast right wing conspiracy". Liberals have been using this idea since the Nixon administration, and the scandals during that administration didn't help silence the notion. Of course, we can't forget the biggest conspiracy of all, that right wing members of the CIA and the defense industry assassinated President Kennedy. There is even this idea in some liberal circles which claims Kennedy was prepared to make known secrets about the Republican Party, and they killed him before he could talk.

The idea of right wing conspiracies really took off during the Clinton administration. The investigation and subsequent impeachment proceedings against President Clinton resulted in liberals nationwide; including the First Lady, claiming the entire impeachment was a conspiracy[1]. The notion took on a life of it's own in 2000 when President George W. Bush won a close election over former Vice President Al Gore. To this day, liberals claim the vote in Florida was rigged and the courts were bought off. Today we have a host of "right wing conspiracies", from people attacking Obama

Administration policies because of his race, to partisan Congressional investigations into the IRS scandal and Benghazi. Liberals see the very notion of the citizens having a right to responsible government as nothing more than a conspiracy against liberals.

Paranoia tends to be one of the tactics liberals use to deflect attention from a topic when they know their other attempts are failing. The closer the public gets to the truth the more likely liberals are to claim they are the victims of a conspiracy. Benghazi is a perfect example of this. First liberals claimed the attack happened because of a horrible video[2], then it was a misunderstanding, and now liberals claim it's nothing more than a "witch hunt"[3]. Liberals seem oblivious to the fact that U.S. citizens died serving their country. They seem unconcerned that lies have been heaped on top of other lies to prevent the public from knowing the truth.

One of the favorite targets for liberal's paranoia is voting. Liberals insist that stronger voter registration is a conspiracy against everyone. It's meant to deter voters because it causes people to show identification. It's a right wing conspiracy to keep minorities from voting because minorities somehow can't show identification[4] [5]. Nothing could be further from the truth. The goal is to make sure our elections are open to all citizens who are legally eligible to vote. In some cases the identification system actually helps to prevent people from being denied the ability to vote. I went to vote in a primary in few years back. The woman who was checking voter registration accidently mistook my name for one of my neighbors and insisted I had already voted. As a result of being required to show government issued identification the mistake was corrected and I was allowed to vote. Unfortunately, liberals want to hide those stories from the public and continue with the lies about decreased voter turn out due to these laws and individuals not having access to identification. The irony of this supposed conspiracy is that the Affordable Care Act requires patients to show identification at the doctor's office before being treated.

When all else fails, the liberals simply turn their paranoia against conservatives. Whenever conservatives begin to point out the unethical or illegal activity liberals are involved in, the liberals label the conservative as "conspiracy theorists". If you actually believe the U.S. citizens deserve to know the truth about our government, then the liberals claim you're a conspiracy theorist. Labeling a conservative a "conspiracy theorist" is the liberal's second favorite tactic to discredit their opponents, the first being to label someone as a racist.

Liberals have been using the conspiracy theorist label for decades. Years ago conservatives began to voice concerns about the Gulf of Tonkin incident and what really happened. Some claimed the entire incident was fabricated to justify the U.S. becoming more involved in Vietnam. Liberals began claiming this was a conspiracy theory. Now we have evidence which indicates the incident really didn't take place[6]. Similarly, when conservative groups began to complain about discriminatory actions by the IRS, liberals instantly claimed conspiracy theorists making up lies to attack the Obama Administration. As more information comes to light, the truth is clearly showing the theory wasn't a conspiracy but a fact. We had a similar situation with the NSA. Conservatives began voicing concerns about a government program spying on the phone calls of U.S. citizens. Liberals claimed these were conspiracy theories developed by mentally unstable conservatives. As more facts are revealed, the more we learn about the full extent of the spying program[7]. Clearly it wasn't a conspiracy theory.

It's amazing how easily the dysfunctional liberal brain can go from insisting they are the target of a conspiracy by conservatives and yet ridicule them as conspiracy theorists for pointing out actual issues. Conservatives are supposedly engaged in a massive conspiracy to prevent illegal immigrants from entering the United States. Yet when conservatives point out the lengths liberals go to in helping illegal immigrants to violate our nation's laws, the liberals claim it's a crazy conspiracy theory. Only an ideology born of drug addiction would display this level of illogical and paranoid thinking.

When claiming anyone who doesn't agree with them is a conspiracy theorist doesn't work, liberals will take to denying the existence of the problem. Denial is a powerful force in all people's live, be they an addict or not. Anyone who has participated in an intervention has experienced the power denial has over the life of an addicted person. In dealing with these individuals, I often found myself confronted with denial. Offenders would deny they committed a crime and they often denied having a problem with drugs and alcohol. In some cases they would even deny they were in a correctional facility because they had been found guilty by the courts. A person cannot begin to deal with any issue as long as they are in denial about the issue existing. The first step in most treatment programs is for the addict to admit they have a problem, thereby removing denial.

The power of denial goes far beyond addiction. Denial is at its core a problem of the soul. As a Christian I know I am saved by the redemptive blood of Jesus Christ. However, to achieve this saving grace I must accept Christ in faith and repent of my sins. Denial and repentance are like oil and water, they simply don't mix. If an individual is in denial of committing a sin, then how can they ask forgiveness of the sin? Satan believed himself to be equal to God and was in denial of God's omnipotent nature. There is an old saying "God helps those who help themselves" meaning those who accept their sin nature, stop denying it and ask forgiveness in the name of Jesus Christ will receive forgiveness and eternal life.

This is the nature of the denial we find within the liberal mindset. There is no reasoning with liberals, they simply deny the truth. When the stories of the IRS targeting conservative groups first surfaced the Obama Administration was in complete denial about the entire situation[8]. Liberals once again claimed the investigation was a "witch hunt"[9]. Surely the Obama Administration doesn't think the public so stupid as to believe this is an innocent coincidence. Instead of taking responsibility for what has occurred, liberals look to fit their detractors with tin foil hats.

Unfortunately, the IRS scandal is simply one in a long string of denials liberals have claimed to clear issues involving poor policy decisions. From Operation Fast and Furious, to the waiting lists at the Veterans Administration, to the Department of Justice seizing journalist's phone records and even the NSA spying on world leaders, there is evidence showing the Obama Administration had some prior knowledge, yet they continue to deny knowing about any of it. This seems to go beyond typical "plausible deniability" which occurs in politics. This is also very different from how conservatives deal with these types of issues. Republican presidents have tended to be more accepting of fault verses denying any involvement. Case in point would be President Nixon's resignation. Where Nixon took responsibility for what happened under his watch, Obama blamed an internet video for Benghazi.

Paranoia and denial aren't normal, whether it's an addict who believes people are out to get them or a liberal politician who believes a legitimate government investigation is a witch hunt. The very fact that liberals believe their enemies are out to get them is indicative of the truly disturbed nature of the liberal mindset. The mindset which leads to paranoid thinking is not conducive to developing bipartisan solutions to problems. How can conservatives ever hope to develop solutions to the serious problems plaguing our nation when the individuals on the other side of the aisle believe they are being targeted as part of a conspiracy or deny the problems exist at all? Furthermore, can anyone work with the liberals when they are determined to take revenge for these illogical conspiracies by conspiring to attack their political enemies? This level of paranoia and denial is not only unhealthy for an individual but also for our nation's political system.

Study Guide:

1: Can you think of a time where liberal's paranoia created problem for the public?
2: How did you feel about the display of paranoia?
3: What are some of the reasons liberals deny facts?
4: What was the goal of the liberal denial?
5: Did the paranoia or denial lead to a greater level of control?
6: What could have been done to minimize the effect of both paranoia and denial?

Chapter 7:
Hyper Defense and Intimidation

It has been my experience in dealing with addicts that they tend to get overly sensitive to any perceived insult against them. Many an addict has ended up in jail because they got into a fight over something the rest of us would let pass without another thought. On one of my first days working in corrections I had to de-escalate a situation in which an offender took to the common area of his housing unit and began threatening the other offenders, trying to intimidate them because he was missing a sock. The offender was responsible for doing his own laundry and the only person responsible for the missing sock was himself. However, he perceived the missing sock to be an insult perpetrated by the other offenders living in his housing unit. He was so convinced of the nonexistent insult that he wanted to intimidate everyone he could to preserve his identity and was willing to fight everyone in the housing unit over it. The sock was eventually found, where it had fallen, behind the clothes washer.

This same hyper defensive condition and intimidation tactics found in addicts is also seen in liberals. There are many areas where hyper defensiveness and intimidation are found, particularly in regards to racial and environmental issues. However, the degree of defensiveness and intimidation found in liberals towards Christianity is far worse than any other issue. Liberals want to destroy Christianity and will stop at nothing to accomplish this goal. I'm not sure liberals actually find Christianity to be offensive in any way. After all, what is so offensive about God sending his only Son to die for your sins so you can have eternal life? Liberals find the end result of Christian beliefs offensive. Like the middle class, Christianity gives people hope for a better tomorrow. People who live with hope in their lives are generally unwilling to throw off the "chains of oppression" and fight as cannon fodder for the liberal elite.

The hyper defensive and intimidation tactics liberals use to attack Christianity vary, but generally follow a similar format. The liberal establishment will pick a very polarizing issue which they know is important to the Christian faith. After picking the issue, liberals will use the mainstream media outlets to demonize and ridicule conservative Christian beliefs. The goal is to shame and emotionally traumatize

Christians into abandoning their faith. As more liberal "Christian" groups begin to show support for the liberal agenda, the media pressure will be increased. The eventual goal will be to gain enough public support through normalcy bias to pass legislation outlawing the Christian belief. There are three areas in public policy where liberals are currently using these tactics: abortion, homosexual rights, and teaching evolution. Having already discussed the abortion issue I'll be focusing on homosexuality and evolution for examples here.

While attending college I wanted to major in anthropology and as a result I spent a considerable amount of time studying evolutionary theory. After all of the classes were over, all of the tests passed and all of the research papers written, I came to a conclusion: human evolution is nonsense! Don't get me wrong here; there is some truth to evolution. What Charles Darwin wrote about in his book has some element of truth to it[1]. There is proverbial mountain of evidence proving animals adapt to their environments through genetic modification. However, a moth changing it's coloring to better camouflage itself from predators is a far cry from a creature crawling out of the water and evolving into human beings.

There are certain traits required in human anatomy to walk on two legs[2]. For example you need forward looking eyes to see where you are going, your head must be situated on top of the spinal column and a double arched foot to bear the load of your body's weight. Ask someone who has broken the arch of their foot how difficult it is to walk. All of these are a matter of mechanics. The human body must have these traits to walk upright. Unfortunately, anthropologists and biologists are declaring fossil specimens they find to be bipedal when they don't even display 10% of these required traits. It's altogether possible for these fossil remains to be from a creature related to another primate.

To make matters worse, the conclusions scientists make about human evolution is based on a very small sample size of fossil remains when compared to the total number of humans who have lived on Earth since the dawn of time. This is the statistical equivalent of flipping a quarter in the air, having it land heads up and then declaring the quarter will always land heads up when it is flipped. We know statistically that a coin flip has a 50-50 chance of landing on a particular side. However, when utilizing a very small sample size, the conclusions can be skewed to provide the evidence needed to prove a particular point of view. Thus is the case with human evolutionary theory where the sample size is so small by comparison as to render it far less than statistically significant. This is where we must distinguish between hard sciences such as statistics and pseudo-sciences such as human evolution. Hard sciences are based in facts which can be demonstrated multiple times. You can prove gravity exists by holding a baseball in your hand and dropping it. No matter how many times you do so, on any piece of land on the face of the Earth, if you release the baseball gravity will pull it down. On the other hand, human evolutionary theory seems to change every three months and there are few tests to prove the viability of the facts.

Having explained all of this, liberals will want to intimidate me for insisting they are wrong. I will be called wrong headed, stupid, or naïve for believing God created humanity. They have no hard evidence to prove God didn't create humanity. However, the idea of God creating life and giving humanity hope is so dangerous to the liberal ideology that liberals get hyper-defensive whenever it's mentioned. Liberals will even take to calling conservatives "subhuman" whenever they feel threatened by the truth. The fact is the liberals push for the teaching of evolutionary theory as a way of introducing the idea that some people are genetically superior to others. It's shocking to realize how many known evolutionary theorists have written articles which appeared in magazines promoting disgusting racial superiority ideology. The liberal elite want the public to believe they are "evolutionarily superior" and the rest of us are "subhuman". As a result, we should allow the liberal elite to make all of the rules and follow in lockstep with what they want.

The epitome of liberal hyper-defensiveness and intimidation is seen in the issue of homosexuality. The tiniest of perceived insult to the homosexual community sets liberals into rage. The liberal elite will turn their political weapons against any Christian who claims homosexuality is a sin with the intent of intimidating Christians to silence. There really isn't any doubt about homosexuality being a sin, the Bible is very clear on this issue[3]. However, homosexuality isn't any worse a sin than any other. The reason liberals want people to believe homosexuality is not a sin is to discredit Christianity and with it the sense of hope which comes with salvation through Jesus Christ. Liberalism believes any idea which gives people hope, other than the liberal ideology, is to be destroyed. The replacement of the Christian faith was the purpose behind the campaign posters featuring the word "HOPE" below a portrait of Barack Obama. The posters were meant to deify Obama and create a subconscious connection for the public to see Obama and the liberal ideology as the source of hope and not Jesus Christ.

The liberal hyper-defensiveness regarding homosexuality provides an excellent window into the true mindset of liberalism and the intimidation tactics it involves. In this context, the liberal elite believe as a result of their evolved superiority, they have the ability to dictate the rights of other people. The growing war on Christianity being waged by the liberals provides ample proof of this. It has almost become a rite of passage for young liberals to attack the Christian faith in the United States. In fact, this is much worse than simple attacks, it is an attempt to exterminate the Christian faith.

In 1988 the United States Senate ratified the Convention on the Prevention and Punishment of the Crime of Genocide. To truly understand the lengths liberals have gone to in denying Christians rights we need to look at Article II of the treaty:

> In the present Convention, genocide means any of the following acts

committed with intent to destroy, in whole or in part, a national, ethnical, racial or religious group, as such:

(b) Causing serious bodily or mental harm to members of the group[4];

Can it not be argued the current actions attempting to shame Christians into accepting homosexuality is in effect an attempt to inflict mental harm on members of the Christian faith with the goal of destroying the faith in its current form? By the letter of the treaty, the crime of attempted act of genocide is being perpetrated against Christians by liberals in the U.S. everyday.

The actions of the Obama Administration make this issue all the more perplexing. Numerous times throughout his presidency, Barack Obama has cited international obligations when engaging in questionable actions. President Obama took military action in Libya without Congressional approval in the name of international obligation[5]. President Obama was willing to go to war in Syria without approval because Syria violated the Chemical Weapons Treaty again in the name of international obligation[6]. The Obama Administration has used various executive orders and other political slight of hand to force the provisions of gun control and environmental treaties on the U.S. citizens when those treaties have never been ratified by the U.S. Senate[7] [8].

Not only do liberals choose when to uphold international obligations at home, they simply ignore them abroad if it's needed to fulfill their objectives. President Obama has provided weapons to rebels in Syria where the Al-Nusra Front, a segment of the Syrian rebellion[9], slaughtered dozens of Christians in the Western Syrian town of Sadad[10] [11]. The Obama Administration has actively supported the Muslim Brotherhood in Egypt who has committed countless crimes against the Coptic Christian community there[12]. The Obama Administration has made little effort to intervene on behalf of Christian U.S. citizens being held in Iran and North Korea. Not only is the Obama Administration ignoring their international obligation to stop these crimes as required by the Genocide Convention, but in some cases they are providing support to the groups who are committing the crimes.

I'm sure the far left will take issue with my use of the term genocide. Liberals will claim I'm insulting victims of genocide or claim it's simply hyperbole meant to elicit fear and anger among the conservative base. The liberal elite will probably even refer to me in private as a naïve "subhuman" with no idea what I'm talking about. However, in looking at the definition provided in the Convention on the Prevention and Punishment of the Crime of Genocide, I believe genocide is the proper word for the actions liberals are taking against Christians. There can be little doubt the liberal elite has created in the Obama Administration a genocidal regime bent on the destruction of the Christian faith.

Hyper defensiveness and intimidation are hallmarks of addict behavior and of the liberal mindset. Liberals will look for the slightest provocation to justify intimidating anyone who dissents with the liberal ideology. The goal is to silence anyone who looks to educate the public to the true will of liberalism. Knowledge and hope are the two greatest weapons against the destructive liberal ideology, and as a result liberals will stop at nothing to destroy these threats.

Study Questions:

1: Can you think of a time where you saw liberals display hyper defensiveness?
2: How did liberals look to intimidate others as a result?
3: What was the goal of the intimidation?
4: Did they achieve their goal?
5: Did the intimidation lead to a greater level of control?
6: What could have been done to prevent the intimidation?

Chapter 8:
The Law is Irrelevant

While working in corrections, I dealt with addicts all the time who didn't believe the law should apply to them. On one occasion, while driving a transportation van I dealt with an offender who was on work release and had failed to arrive at his transportation pick-up point. As I was preparing to drive away from the pick-up point I saw the offender running across a busy street in the middle of traffic and almost cause an accident to get to the van. Beyond not being at his pick-up point on time, I also observed the offender violating three city ordinances. Upon returning to the facility I wrote my report about the incident and the offender complained because I mentioned he had violated the facility rules which included not breaking local laws while out in the community. According to the offender those local laws could not be applied to him because I wasn't a police officer in that jurisdiction. No matter how many times I tried to explain this situation to him, he could not understand that by me observing him violate the law it placed him in violation of the facility rules. Based on this offender's logic, if law enforcement officer for the jurisdiction where the crime is committed does not see you commit a crime you can't be charged with it.

I had honestly forgotten all about the incident until I was watching the news on May 19th 2013 when White House Spokesman Dan Pfefiffer appeared on ABC News's "This Week with George Stephanopoulos" to discuss the IRS targeting of conservative groups. Mr. Pfefiffer famously stated, "I can't speak to the law. The law is irrelevant…"[1] I had an immediate flashback to the offender who refused to acknowledge the law applied to him. Whether it's liberal members of Congress committing crimes[2] [3] or Barack Obama doing an end run around Congress to bomb Libya[4], the liberal elite don't seem to think the law applies to them.

While there have been a number of egregious displays of this disrespect for the rule of law, I'm just going to site a few examples. One example is the Obama Administration's assassination of U.S. citizen Anwar al-Awlaki. Now according to all available evidence, Anwar al-Awlaki had abused his position as a U.S. citizen to help terrorist groups plot to kill fellow U.S. citizens. I doubt there are many U.S. citizens who don't feel that he should have faced the appropriate punishment for his crimes. Unfortunately, he was denied the right to due process of law, even if it had meant trial in absentia. Instead, the Obama Administration looked for ways around the law prohibiting the murder of U.S. citizens on foreign soil. The memorandum produced by the Obama Administration to justify their action holds an interesting line.

To quote from the memorandum:

> In some instances, therefore, the better view of a criminal prohibition may well be that Congress meant to distinguish those persons who are acting pursuant to public authority, at least in some circumstances, from those who are not, even if the statute by terms does not make that distinction express[5].

The Obama Administration then tries to defend this position by arguing that criminal law does not provide for police officers to violate traffic laws when in pursuit of a suspect. The argument is absurd since every state in the nation has statues in place allowing individuals operating emergency vehicles to operate them as necessary to perform the required duty.

What is more disturbing is how the Obama Administration believes Congress intended to allow the President to assassinate U.S. citizens on foreign soil, but they simply never "make that distinction express". The law in question here is Title 18 U.S.C. Section 1119 and while this law has been affirmed by Congress on more than one occasion the most recent was in 1994. In 1993, this law was included as part of House Resolution 3355 under the title "Violent Crime Control and Law Enforcement Act of 1994[6]" on October 26th and was scheduled with the Judiciary Committee. On November 3, 1993, after 40 minutes of debate, H.R. 3355 was approved by the House of Representatives and was sent to the Senate on November 4th. On November 19th the Senate approved an amended version of H.R. 3355 and requested a conference with the House to compile a compromised bill. H.R. 3355 was in conference committee from approximately April 21st 1994 until August 21st 1994 when the committee report was finally presented and the final draft of the bill approved by the House. The bill was approved by the Senate on August 22nd 1994 and signed into law by President Clinton on September 13th 1994. Between October 26th 1993 and August 21st 1994, elements of H.R. 3355 were debated on the floor of the House of Representatives on 15 different occasions for a total of 15 hours and 20 minutes of debates over various provisions of this bill[7].

Now the Obama Administration expects us to believe Congress intended to give the President of the United States the authority to assassinate

U.S. citizens on foreign soil, but in almost 15 and a half hours of debate they simply forgot to express the idea. In fact, on July 26th 1994 there was a debate held on the House floor regarding which factors should be considered when applying the death penalty[8]. It would seem the perfect time for discussing the application of capital punishment against a U.S. citizen without regards for due process would have been during the aforementioned debate, and yet no mention was made. I simply don't understand how Congress could forget to discuss an idea of that magnitude. Clearly, the evidence that the Obama Administration is claiming justifies the killing of a U.S. citizen, is ridicules.

Liberals often ignore the law in the pursuit of their destructive goals. The Obama Administration exemplifies this tendency in their use of executive orders. From gun control to environmental regulations, President Obama has made it a point throughout his presidency to disregard the wishes of the citizens and ignore Congress when he feels the whim to do so. Executive orders were never intended to be a means of making policy. Think of executive orders as a memorandum from a company's CEO telling the company's employees how to handle certain situations. Executive orders are intended to be used as a means of providing a quick fix to handling the mandates Congress has placed on the federal government.

Unfortunately, this is not how the Obama Administration utilizes executive orders. Instead, they see executive orders as a means of pushing forward their policy agenda without any regard for the U.S. Constitution. Some of the most notable executive orders President Obama has issued were the 23 orders regarding gun control he signed in January 2013[9]. Two of the executive orders in question deal with research and reviewing the requirements for gun safety devices. The U.S. Supreme Court already dealt with the issue of gun safety devices in their District of Columbia v. Heller decision[10]. The Obama Administration seems to ignore, not only Congress but the nation's highest court, when it pleases them. It will be interesting to see how President Obama responds to the high court's unanimous decision against his recess appointments to the National Labor Board[11].

When not ignoring U.S. Supreme Court decisions, President Obama was creating mandates for state governments and the health care industry. There are two problems with these types of executive orders. First, the President of the United States does not have the authority to unilaterally require state governments or private businesses to take any action outside of a national emergency, and then only if the directives are covered under the National Defense Authorization Act. Secondly, the executive orders in question require tax payer money to fund new programs. Executive orders were never intended to be used to direct money to be spent on a particular government program or to start a new government program. The U.S. Constitution is very clear regarding the procedures required to create new spending by the federal government. The bill must be introduced into the House of Representatives first, then after House approval it is sent to the Senate and finally to the President for a signature. This is not the first time liberals in Washington D.C. have displayed a difficult time understanding how this system works. The Affordable Care Act began as a bill in the U.S. Senate and not the House, leading many to cry foul to its legality.

Generally speaking, the liberal elite tend to view the law as a game and they are constantly trying to find new and innovative ways to play the game. The goal of the game from the liberal perspective is to gain as much power as possible and by any means necessary. Liberals are very similar to the Pharisees of the Bible. In Matthew 23:4 Christ provides a description of the Pharisees which is fitting of modern liberals when he said "For they bind heavy burdens and grievous to be borne, and lay them on men's shoulders; but they themselves will not move them with one of their fingers."[12]

This concept of irrelevance of the law has at its root the desire to rationalize the means of controlling the world around them. For the drug addict, the need is to rationalize the crimes being committed in order to obtain more drugs. The drug addict believes on some level that it's okay to steal from others since they are hurting and needing drugs to feel better. I've even seen situations where the addict goes so far as to rationalize themselves being a victim and the crime they are committing is a means of justice. Liberals operate on a very similar principle where the end is rationalized to justify the means. Liberals want the rest of us being forced to buy into the healthcare exchanges, but they rationalize the exclusion of some liberal groups by claiming they aren't part of the "young invincibles" for whom the system was designed. Liberals want to take guns away from citizens while at the same time rationalizing their need for protection because of their high profile position. The law is irrelevant as long as they can rationalize their own actions.

From refusing to take part in government programs, to killing U.S. citizens, modern liberalism and drug addiction look very similar in their desire to rationalize the legalities to justify their own immoral or unethical actions. In the addiction controlled mind of the liberal elite, they rationalize the right to break the law because they are evolutionarily superior to all of us "sub humans". However, as the cold truth of reality begins to creep in, the liberal ability to rationalize beings to fade and the justification collapses like a poorly built house of cards. It's at this point the addict mindset displays it's most dangerous aspect.

Study Questions:

1: Can you think of a time where you saw liberals violate the law?
2: How did liberals rationalize the illegal action?
3: What was the goal of the illegal action?
4: Did they achieve their goal?
5: Did the action result in a greater level of control?
6: What could have been done to hold liberals accountable under the law?

Chapter 9: Attacking

Violence is almost a constant in a correctional facility. Offenders are continually picking fights with other offenders and in some cases offenders even lash out at correctional staff. It's one of the hazards of the job you deal with everyday when you go to work in such an environment. There is a mantra amongst corrections staff, "I'm going home". No matter what happens you remember your primary goal is to make sure you go home at the end of the shift. While violence is not particular to drug addiction, physical and verbal attacks tend to be one of the most disturbing aspects of addiction. Regardless of the substance being used, all drugs have the ability to cause an individual to act in a violent manner. Despite the notion of certain drugs, such as marijuana, not causing violent reactions; this is simply untrue. I've known of habitual marijuana users who were convicted of murder. Addiction causes people to change their behavior and do things they might not do otherwise. Where a person without any addiction might be calm, once a foreign substance is introduced into their body their underlying tendencies come to the surface. If an individual has underlying anger and aggression issues, those issues will come out when their inhibitions are removed by drug use.

Aggression and attacking are generally the last desperate attempts for both the addict and the liberal elite. Attacking their opponents is usually reserved for situations where all of the other tactics discussed up to this point have failed to work. Attacking isn't always in the form of a physical attack; it can also be social or even legal. One of the favorite tools for these attacks in the political arena is the use of mass media. Liberals see firearms as one of the major impediments to their goal for control. Liberals have tried lying about the number of gun related deaths in the U.S. Liberals have tried confusing the issue by claiming U.S. citizens own "assault rifles". The Obama Administration has even gone so far as disregarding the law to enact executive orders in pursuit of gun control. We've even seen the Department of Justice use intimidation tactics against financial institutions who deal with firearms retailers[1]. None of these tactics have worked, so the next step is to use the media to attack the idea of gun ownership. We'll begin seeing television programs claiming patriots are evil and firearms have no place in a civilized society. We'll begin seeing legal attacks against firearms retailers, in an attempt to prevent them from doing business.

This is not the first time we will have seen the liberals use these same tactics against their conservative opponents. The ongoing scandal regarding IRS investigations of conservative groups followed this same plan. As the Tea Party grew in size and popular support, liberals became concerned about the growing influence. As a result, liberals began telling lies about the Tea Party being full of racists and domestic terrorists[2]. As those lies failed to sway public opinion, liberals began to confuse the issues Tea Party supporters were championing, such as gun rights. As it became clear the Tea Party movement was gaining momentum, liberals looked to intimidate and attack conservative groups by using IRS agents to harass them[3]. Now we're learning the true scale of this attack, the targets of liberal aggression even included Christian charity organizations and conservative members of the U.S. Senate[4].

Sadly, these kinds of politically motivated attacks are becoming a common tactic used by liberals to force conservative voices from the public arena. The types of political attacks used by liberals are designed to have a negative impact on the free speech rights of the public. What person wants to give money to support a political cause when they have to fear repercussions from the opponents of the group they are supporting? Where, exactly, does this end? How many conservatives will lose money and even employment before liberals are held accountable for this type of harassment? We have already observed businesses refusing to take part in homosexual weddings being targeted not only in the courts but by government entities[5]. These attacks are meant to have the effect of forcing citizens from being part of their government. Where President Lincoln believed our nation was a "government of the people, by the people and for the people[6]", Liberals seem intent to eliminate the people from any participation in government. Even now the government is providing grants to fund programs designed to track "hate speech" and other "subversive" comments about the government on the internet[7]. The U.S. government is using tax dollars to stifle the free speech of U.S. citizens and no one seems to care.

Liberals have used attack and intimidation tactics since they first appeared on the U.S. political scene. The first appearance of a melding between modern liberalism and the Democratic Party seems to have occurred in the 1880s. During the years after the Civil War, there was a sharp increase in immigration from central Europe, mainly the area now referred to as Germany. As discussed in Chapter 1, many of these immigrants came to the U.S. having already been exposed to Marx's liberal ideology and they took those views into the workplace. The result was the first attempts by liberals seeking to establish labor unions and enact social reforms. The one impediment to the establishment of labor unions was the readily available pool of African American laborers. In the wake of the Civil War and emancipation, there were large numbers of unemployed African Americans in the former Confederate states. Employers had no reason to deal with labor unions when they could just as easily hire African Americans to do the same jobs, sometime for lower wages. This infuriated liberals who saw the actions of employers as an attempt to deprive them of their much sought after workers revolt.

The result was liberals collaborating with groups such as the Ku Klux Klan to attack and intimidate African Americans to keep them from crossing the union's picket lines. Liberals continued to use racist hate groups into the 1960 when it became politically unacceptable, at which time they switched to the Nation of Islam. Liberals continued their relationship with the Nation of Islam until just after the September 11, 2001 terrorist attacks, when again political pressure forced a change. Now liberals have moved to La Rasa, a Hispanic racial superiority group whose name "the race" clearly indicates their true ideology. This is without a doubt one of the most despicable aspects of the liberal ideology. They have no concern for human life if they are not in control of it. Furthermore, it demonstrates their willingness to use any means necessary to control others, including fear and violence.

Liberalism's disregard for human life isn't limited to attacking their political rivals for gain. We have learned over the years how liberals utilize attacking as a means of creating a distraction from other political scandals. In 1998, I remember watching the House of Representatives voting on the articles of impeachment against President Clinton. As the votes were being shown in one corner of the television screen, the opposite corner showed the all too familiar green hued night vision view of Baghdad, Iraq as U.S. warplanes bombed targets related to Saddam Hussein's supposed WMD program[8]. We later learned there were no WMDs in Iraq, which leaves us to wonder what, exactly, President Clinton was bombing. More importantly, since there was nothing there to bomb, was President Clinton putting both innocent Iraqi citizens and U.S. troops in harms way to create a distraction from the impeachment proceedings?

This tactic, sometimes referred to as "waging the dog[9]", has become an all too familiar aspect of liberal foreign policy. President Obama attempted to use this tactic during his drive to attack Syria over the use of the supposed use of chemical weapons. President Obama's insistence on using troops was intended to take attention away from the IRS targeting of Conservative groups and the Benghazi scandal. A similar tactic was used by the Johnson Administration during the 1960's to escalate U.S. involvement in Vietnam. Liberals claimed a U.S. naval vessel was attacked in the Gulf of Tonkin, when the records were later declassified we learned no attack occurred[10]. The Johnson Administration was simply trying to use a foreign war as a distraction from the growing civil rights movement in the U.S. Clearly the tactic didn't work as President Johnson would eventually be forced, by growing public pressure, to sign the Civil Rights Act into law.

The end result for the Johnson Administration is generally true any time liberals take to using attack tactics. The liberal elite resort to these tactics in a last, desperate attempt to maintain power. Furthermore, when liberals utilize these tactics, it has a tendency to get out of control and inflict much more damage then they intended. The biggest fear held by liberal elites is for their true agenda to be disclosed to the public. As long as they can continue the illusion of caring about the masses, they can continue to grow an army to fight their battles for them. Liberals elites will not fight the battles themselves. We see an example of this in the gun control debate. Liberals political leaders will talk about gun confiscation but none of them will be willing to actually go to individual's homes and seize their firearms. Instead, the liberal elite want the police or military to carry out these confiscations. The reason for this is two fold. First, liberals know Second Amendment advocates will not give up their firearms willingly. Attempting to seize firearms from U.S. citizens will lead to a violent response and liberals don't want to be on the receiving end of the response. Secondly, liberals want police and military casualties they can air on the nightly news as proof of how violent armed citizens are and why their guns need to be seized. Both results would benefit the goals of the liberal elite to gain power and control the public. It's simply an added benefit for people to die in the process of the liberal elite achieving these goals.

Violence and attacking is as much a part of the liberal mindset as it is part of the culture of drug use and addiction. The history of modern liberalism is full of examples showing the desire of liberals to fulfill their goals through force and violence. From Chicago's Haymarket Riots to the IRS targeting of conservative groups, liberals have shown us their true nature. During the debate about the Affordable Care Act, opponents of the law were beaten by liberal members of labor unions[11]. Once again, this is the use of attacking their opposition to silence them and infringe upon their First Amendment Rights. Liberals will even take to using these same tactics against dissidents in their own ranks. During the Occupy Wall Street protests we saw reports of violence inside the camps, including beatings, murders and rapes[12].

Violence is, at its core, the result of failure. Liberals attacked Tea Party related groups because they failed to recognize the U.S. citizen's were turning against the liberal ideology. The liberal elite were angry at the Tea Party, seeing them as subhuman pests needing to be exterminated. This same mentality plays out in liberal political ideology, drug addiction or spousal abuse. For the drug addict, it's a failure to control their own life and the realization that they've allowed their addiction to take control which results in them acting out violently against others or even themselves. For the abusive spouse, it's the realization that they have failed to control the relationship, so they act out in violence trying to regain control. For liberals, they come to the point of realizing their failure to gain control of power over the people so they lash out in violence against the groups they see impeding their ability to gain control.

Left unchecked the end result of these violent attacks is almost always one of two possibilities, either prison or death. For the drug addict, the result is either prison or death by overdose or suicide. For the spousal abuser it's either prison or the death of their spouse, which leads to prison also. For liberals, it's either prison for corruption or the death of our nation. This is why it's so important for us to stand up and stop liberalism now before it goes any further. The only way to prevent the death of our great nation is to intervene and stop liberals from carrying out their destructive plans.

Study Questions:

1: Can you think of a time where you saw liberals attack political opponents?
2: How did liberals carry out their attack?
3: What was the goal of the attack?
4: Did they achieve their goal?
5: Did the attack result from a failure by liberals?
6: What could have been done to prevent the attack from occurring?

Chapter 10:
Liberal Elite- The Merchants of Death

Up to this point, I've drawn examples of how the addict mindset and behaviors are manifested within modern liberalism. There is one stark difference between the two. The goal of a drug addict is to acquire their next high. The goal of the liberal elite is to acquire absolute power over humanity. This is where liberalism takes its diabolical turn from just another failed political ideology to an ideology of mass destruction. In its most basic form, liberalism is the combination of populism and a genocidal ideology. The liberal elite will take up whatever beliefs are held by the masses and then corrupt those beliefs to serve their own nefarious goals. The perfect example of this is the mass influx of illegal immigrant children who began flooding the southern U.S. boarder in June 2014. The mainstream media, influenced by liberal elitists, has portrayed the influx as being small children. The truth is, most of these children are adolescents from El Salvador. The more disturbing aspect of this story is the realization that many of these adolescents are members of the infamous "MS-13" street gang[1]. This is a street gang so violent they carry out their crimes in the middle of Washington D.C. in broad daylight only blocks from the FBI headquarters[2]. Despite this realization, many liberals are claiming this is not a crisis, but an opportunity to finally break down the barriers preventing illegal immigrants from becoming part of our society[3]. In reality, the liberal elite are looking to bring in more cannon fodder to increase their numbers to attack conservatives.

The nature of liberalism is very difficult for conservatives to understand. Most voters who identify as liberals fail to understand the ideology they are supporting; they only follow along because of liberalism's popular nature. If you press the typical liberal voter to explain what liberalism actually stands for, you will hear an explanation regarding a vague idea of social justice. In reality, all justice is social on some level since the courts derive their power from the law and the laws are derived from socially acceptable practices. The term social justice is simply a way for liberals to say they don't approve of the law and the society which created those laws. As a result, the concept of social justice leaves the typical liberal voter feeling disenfranchised with the system and more willing to embrace political change, even when the change will be to their detriment.

The liberal concept of social justice has acted as the building block for most of the far left's policy platform for the last 30 years. However, nothing the liberals do is about making society better and justice is the furthest idea from their warped minds. The liberal elite want control over the public and they're simply using the bogus concept of social justice to pursue their goal. There is no length the liberal elite won't go to in order to achieve their goal of control. The desire for control has driven liberalism since its beginning and even today the world is dealing with the horrifying consequences. Once again, this is the liberal elite's continuation of Nietzsche's concept of "will to power".[4]

When you ask the liberal elite about liberalism and social justice you will hear something different. The liberal leadership will talk about social justice in terms of "second and third generation human rights". These are separate from first generations rights as we see in the Bill of Rights. The first generation rights are seen as "negative rights" while second and third generation rights are seen as "positive rights".[5] Second generation rights seek to address social and economic issues revolving around labor unions, welfare and other typically liberal ideas which grew out of Karl Marx's writings. The third generation rights are sometimes referred to as "green rights" as they grew out of the United Nation's Rio Declaration of 1992[6]. These rights often deal with collective rights which are provided to an entire group of people. In looking at the evolution of these three generations of "rights", we see the liberals slowly removing the perceived "negative" rights of the individual and replacing them with the "positive" rights of the collective.

The first of the "third generation rights" listed in the Rio Declaration is the sovereignty of the state[7]. As Christians, we recognize only one sovereign, God. Since liberals see the state as sovereign, they have no use for God. Liberals don't hold to a religion, they see the state as their religion. Remember the discussion of Nietzsche in Chapter One and his idea of God being dead. The liberal idea of "God is dead[8]" and the rise of the sovereignty of the state is a direct result of Nietzsche's teaching. They see themselves having evolved beyond religion and having achieved some type of superhuman status where the rest of us are subhuman. As a result, liberals tend to hold the rest of humanity in disregard. This is why liberals don't understand Thomas Jefferson's belief that humanity is "endowed by their Creator with certain unalienable Rights"[9]. In the liberal mindset only the state can grant rights, and those rights are provided to the collective, and never to the individual.

Liberals see individuals as tools to be used to further their political desire for power. When they have achieved their goals, they simply discard the individuals for others who better serve the cause. This has been seen time and again throughout our nation's history. In fact, this is, in all likelihood, a carry over to modern liberalism from the Democratic Party. From its very beginnings the Democratic Party has been a party of genocide. Starting with President Jackson, the Democratic Party engaged in policies designed to wipe out the Native Americans from this entire continent[10]. From disease infested blankets, to alcohol and forced removal of indigenous populations, the Democratic Party took every opportunity they could find to destroy not only the lives of Native Americans, but their very culture as well.

While trying to wipe out Native Americans, the Democratic Party was also working tirelessly to preserve the horrific institution of slavery. Despite repeated attempts to end slavery, the Democratic Party continued on with the horrific practice, even going so far as to present misleading versions of Bible texts, claiming the scriptures supported slavery[11]. Democrats even took to attacking and intimidating Republican abolitionists fighting to free slaves from southern plantations. When faced with the prospect of failure and the reality of finally losing their slaves in 1861, southern Democrats attacked The United States government and seceded from the Union, sparking the Civil War[12].

In looking at the actions of the Democratic Party in the first century of our nation's existence, it's easy to see why they were so quick to adopt the European concept of liberalism. The tactics being used by liberals and the Democratic Party were very similar and allowed for an easy merging of ideas.

Once we see the merger between European liberalism and the Democratic Party take place, the level of death and destruction brought upon our nation is quickly amplified. By the early 20th Century, liberals had begun to turn back some of the advances conservative Republican administrations had made in the decades after the Civil War[13]. By the time President Theodore Roosevelt left office, the federal work place was desegregated and conservative Republicans had made numerous attempts to pass various civil rights laws since the late 1860s[14]. Unfortunately, liberal Democrats were beginning to make in roads into U.S. politics. The first liberal victories took place with court challenges to desegregation laws in the 1870s. By the time

President Woodrow Wilson took office in 1913, liberals were moving to re-segregate the federal workplace and this was finally accomplished during the Wilson Administration[15].

In the writings of President Wilson, we see the final merging of the liberal ideology and the Democratic Party platform. Wilson's writings reveal an ideology which has merged the Democratic Party's views on slavery and control with the liberal views on labor and economics[16]. Slavery is seen as bad in that it deprived workers of unionization. Wilson writes favorably of other forms of slavery found in South America and sees African Americans as inferior to Europeans[17]. This once again follows along with similar views held by Marx and other early liberal philosophers who saw certain aspects of humanity as being subhuman. The end result of this is seen today in the liberal notion of liberals being evolutionarily superior to the rest of humanity and thus justifying the liberal belief of intellectual superiority. These beliefs have been the justification for liberals to believe the law doesn't apply to them since they are superior to the law.

The end of the Wilson Administration saw a series of horrific crimes committed by liberals against U.S. citizens. African Americans were used in experiments by liberal doctors[18]. African

American and Native American women were sterilized by liberal groups pushing for population control[19]. During the early days of World War 2, Japanese Americans were forced into internment camps by the liberal administration of President Franklin Roosevelt. These and many more examples provide evidence of the true nature of the liberal ideology, and some of these same beliefs are held by liberals today.

When not enslaving humanity, liberals are content to kill massive numbers of humans in the pursuit of power. Over the last 100 years our nation has been involved in five major military conflicts: World War I, World War II, the Korean War, the Vietnam War, and the recent War on Terrorists (Afghanistan and Iraq). Four of those five conflicts began when a liberal Democrat was in the White House. Furthermore, three of those five wars were on some level conflicts between differing far left ideologies. World War II in Europe was the U.S. and Britain (Liberalism) and Russia (Communism) verses Germany (National Socialism). The Korean and Vietnam Wars were both conflicts between Liberalism and Communism. These are all leaves on the same diseased branch of political ideologies, fighting to gain power and impose their specific brand of leftist beliefs on the world.

Over the 100 year period from 1908 to 2008, Liberal Democrats have been President of the United States when 607,011 service men and women have died in military conflicts[20]. By contrast 15,119 service men and women have died when a Conservative Republican has been President[21]. To put this plainly, Republican presidents have been responsible for 2.4% of the U.S. military casualties over the 100 year period. This leaves 97.6% of U.S. military casualties having occurred when a Democrat was in the Oval Office. To break this down to it's most basic form, 34 U.S. citizens died in combat for each day a Democrat served as president during the 100 year period. These statistics should shock every U.S. citizen.

The very history of liberalism in the United States should be enough to convince any voter to avoid the ideology at all cost. This is where conservatives have truly failed this nation, by not teaching our fellow citizens the truth. Liberals want nothing more than for the voting public to be ignorant and enslaved. Conservatives, be it the Republican Party, the Tea Party or other groups, must make it a priority to educate the voting public about the horrors liberalism has brought on our nation. Education is the only way we will ever wrestle our nation free from this century long nightmare.

Study Questions:

1: Can you think of a time where you saw liberals display a different view of human rights?
2: How did liberals rationalize their beliefs?
3: What were the goals of their beliefs and did they achieve those goals?
4: How did their belief make you feel?
5: How did the belief impact other citizens?
6: What can you do to help educate voters about destructive liberal beliefs?

Chapter 11:
Ensuring the Public Trust

As I did in *Null and Void,* I want to provide a plausible solution to the problems our nation is facing. We are at a critical point in our nation's life and if we don't begin to correct some of these issues now we never will be able to. There is a need for a litmus test for determining if government policies are ethical. The purpose of this test is to provide a quick and easy means of determining the amount of damage a perspective law can do to our society and stop the bill from becoming a law in the first place. It is much easier to eliminate the problem before it becomes law than to deal with it after the bill is signed into law. We are finding this out the hard way with the Affordable Care Act. To achieve this goal, I'm proposing a new non-partisan pledge for politicians. The pledge, named The Government Accountability Pledge, will ask political candidates to pledge to withhold any sponsorship, support or votes from any piece of legislation, requiring the spending of taxpayer money, which violates four basic rules for ethical government. Over these next four chapters I will lay out the framework for this new pledge.

The first rule for ethical government is to pass no law which endangers the publics trust. As a public administration student in college, I was taught to do nothing to endanger the public trust. In a democracy, the government's power to govern and make policy comes from the citizens. Without the authority of the citizens, the government is no longer a democracy but a totalitarian regime. Under ideal circumstances, citizens will not give up their rights to a government they don't trust. This is where the previously discussed tactics used by liberals come into play. By confusing the issue, lying, misleading or intimidation, liberals have convinced many U.S. citizens of the need to abandon "first generation rights" in favor of "third generation rights" which provide more control to an increasingly untrustworthy government.

The reasons public trust is important are two fold. First, democratic government can only occur with the consent of the people. Secondly, the elected government needs a form of plausible deniability. As long as the public trusts the government, the elected government can claim to be doing the will of the people. If things go wrong, then the elected government can simply claim they were doing the will of the people and it's the voters who are to blame. The problem is, liberalism doesn't really want to govern by the will of the people since the liberal elite believe themselves to be intellectually superior to the sub-humans. As a result, liberals have no problem jeopardizing the public's trust in the course of achieving their goals.

This situation is further complicated because many public servants are not elected officials. There is no way for the public to determine who should serve as police officers, firefighters, IRS agents, or most other government jobs. The citizens are at the mercy of public servants to make the right decision. So what happens when the public loses faith in the ability of the government to make the proper decision? For the answer to this question, we need look no further than the current lack of trust most U.S. citizens have in our nation's government. The Obama Administration has provided multiple examples of this as one unelected government employee after another has been implicated in the growing number of scandals. In typical liberal fashion, the Obama Administration has used unelected government workers to take the fall for unethical and illegal activities while leaving the President able to claim no knowledge of the incidents.

As these scandals continue to grow in number, there is an interesting transformation which begins to take shape. As the government takes on a more corrupt appearance, the public wants to distance itself from the government. As the public loses trust in the government, there is a corresponding loss of public engagement. This decrease in engagement is seen in lower approval ratings and lower voter turnout during elections. As this decrease in trust and engagement continues, there develops an "us against them" mentality within both the public sector employees and the public itself. We see this mentality in the actions of government officials who take a very heavy handed approach to dealing with the public. We also see this in certain parts of the public with the notion of the government being against the citizens. Both of these are valid feelings as the government's heavy handed approach creates the appearance of the government being against the citizens. This leads to more problems and left unchecked will result in violence between the government and the citizens.

The "us against them" mentality is extremely divisive and serves no constructive purpose in our society. The only people benefiting from this mentality are the liberals seeking to "divide and conquer" the populace. As mentioned in chapter nine, liberals will look to cause violent conflicts as an excuse to take more individual rights. The violence will act as a rallying cry for the restriction of rights and the establishment of new third generation collective rights as outlined in the 1992 Rio Declaration[1]. We are already seeing scandals which serve to highlight why policies, which violate the public trust, are so dangerous.

The most prominent example in the news today is the NSA spying program. There is very little evidence to prove the NSA programs have helped to stop acts of terrorism. However, in the process of not stopping terrorism, the government has been collecting information on U.S. citizens[2]. The more information we learn about this program the more we realize how out of control our government has become. The NSA program was clearly not limited to individuals who posed a risk to the United States. After all, the program was spying on our allies as well as our citizens. The damage to the public trust is done, regardless of what the Obama Administration claims was their purpose.

These scandals cause the public to begin questioning their ability to elect a truly responsive government. As the scandals pile up, the public can't continue to blame the politicians when it was the public who voted those same politicians into office. Slowly but surely the public will begin to take one of two cognitive paths. The first is to stop voting and become disenfranchised by the failure of government. The second is to blame themselves for the problems and accept any solution offered up by progressive liberals. Both paths work towards the goal of liberal control of the populace. With fewer people voting in elections, there will be less need for resources to sell the lies. The individuals who are willing to accept the public being responsible for the problem are already buying into to collectivist mindset liberals are pushing on the public. Both paths allow for the easy implementation of a government as defined under the 1992 Rio Declaration[3].

The answer to this problem is to hold elected officials accountable for enacting laws which endanger the public trust. This is best accomplished by the voters, who refuse to vote for any elected official, who supports these types of laws. Furthermore, politicians who stand up against these types of destructive policies should be praised and supported by the voters. By asking political candidates to publicly declare their support for the Government Accountability Pledge, the voters will know which candidates to support and which to vote against. If a politician decides to support a law which endangers the public trust, they will face the consequences of those actions in the form of reduced voter support.

Study Questions:

1. Can you think of a policy which endangers the public trust?
2. Can you think of ways liberals use these dangerous policies to their advantage?
3. How do you think the candidate pledge would help resolve the issue?

Chapter 12:
The Rule of Law

Like most other nations in the world, our nation functions under the rule of law; the basic concept whereby all people regardless of race, creed, religion, status in society or any other factor are treated equally before the law. In essence, the law is to be blind to all factors, exclusive of the law itself and the facts presented before the courts. The legal system also operates under the premise that a party cannot gain advantage or profit from violating the law. While this concept is closely tied to endangering the public trust, there are some differences. Policies which jeopardize the rule of law will always endanger the public trust, but the opposite is not always true. For example, a policy which helps to erode the public trust, such as giving preferential treatment to certain business groups, does not necessarily violate the rule of law.

The issue of illegal immigration has been in the news a lot recently and part of the current debate regarding immigration reform has been the issue of amnesty. Providing a path for illegal aliens to obtain citizenship is not only a violation of the public trust but also a violation of the rule of law. The U.S. government extends opportunities for legal immigration and citizenship as part of maintaining the public trust. However, amnesty represents an attempt by the government to create a way for individuals to gain citizenship despite breaking the law. It is unethical for the government to create policies which reward individuals for breaking the law. Bank robbers are not allowed to keep the money they steal and mass murderers are not allowed to write tell all books. Police departments are not allowed to use illegally obtain evidence in court. The whole premise here is to prohibit criminals from profiting from ill gotten gains.

The underlying problems with policies which violate the rule of law are the long term effects. These types of policies are often times used to set perilous legal precedents with sometimes far reaching consequences. Once governments begin to disregard the rule of law, there is no safety for its citizens. What starts out as allowing illegal immigrants an easy path to citizenship can become an excuse for a judge to ignore the Fourth and Fifth Amendment protections of a defendant in a court of law. If the law no longer applies to policy, then what else does the law not apply to? Quickly, the system can spiral into a dictatorship with little transparency and no voice for the public. Clearly this would be the worst case scenario, but with the propensity governments have for violating the most basic of civil rights, it's a scenario citizens would be foolish not to consider possible.

The more likely scenario is what we see playing out with the Obama Administration. In Chapter 8, I discussed the ways liberals seek to avoid the law in pursuit of their goals. Liberals have come to expect the public to look the other way when they violate the law because they have been developing policies designed to violate the rule of law for years. In the liberal mindset, we are already so far down this slippery slope to the point there they believe "the law is irrelevant".[1] The Obama Administration didn't just wake up on the morning of May 19th 2013 and decide the best way out of a scandal was to declare "the law is irrelevant".[2] The statement was the result of a long series of events where the Obama Administration, and other liberal factions prior to this one, violated the rule of law. Before the statement was made, the Obama Administration had already made unconstitutional recess appointments to the labor board[3], passed numerous executive orders and at some points completely disregarded the Constitution altogether.

Liberals seem to believe it's acceptable to pass legislation and enact policies which violate the rule of law because; in their eyes, the end justifies the means. However, the end they are seeking is not in the best interest of the citizens, but to help the liberal elite gain control. One of the best examples of liberals attempting to use policies which violate the rule of law for their own gain is in their attempts to reduce the requirements for voting. We know the law allows for all citizens to vote as long as they meet certain basic requirements. This being the case, it only makes sense to ensure individuals who are casting votes are eligible to do so. Unfortunately, liberals see these voter registration laws as an obstacle to achieve the votes they need to get elected and as a result liberals believe voter fraud is justified since it helps them achieve their goals.

In a larger sense, the rule of law is at the heart of our society. Every society which existed since the time of Hammurabi has possessed some form of codified rules which governed the interactions of the society. It is a truly disturbing development to see liberals in our nation openly defying the laws in the pursuit of their own destructive agenda. However, while this disregard for the rule of law is disturbing, it's hardly surprising. As I explained in Chapter 8, the activity we are seeing from liberals in this regard is very similar to the actions of a drug addict and is a natural extension of the addict ideology from which liberalism was born.

The best method for U.S. citizens to fight violations of the rule of law is with the law it self. This might seem counterintuitive since liberals are already breaking the law. However, the goal here is to place as many barriers as possible between the destructive tactics liberals are using and the goals they hope to achieve. In the corrections field there is a saying for dealing with offenders; firm, fair, and consistent. The offender got to a correctional facility by breaking the law, so imposing more laws on them will not serve as a deterrent. If rules were a deterrent, I would never have written a disciplinary report for a violation. The goal is to limit the damage which can be done and provide a form of legal sentry system to alert when a problem exists. By imposing sanctions for minor rule violations, we hope to prevent major violations from occurring.

The Government Accountability Pledge would ask candidates to withhold any support and take a stand against legislation designed to violate the rule of law. The goal is to prevent these destructive pieces of legislation from becoming law and to highlight individuals who support such bills. Once again, this is about holding elected officials responsible for the legislation they pass. If a member of Congress votes for a bill designed to violate the rule of law, then that member of Congress should be held accountable at the ballot box by all citizens. There should be a form of public shaming which comes along with supporting bills which violate the rule of law. Violating the rule of law for personal gain should be seen as the shameful behavior it is and until we begin to highlight this problem it will continue.

Study Questions:

1. Can you think of a policy which violates the rule of law?
2. Can you think of ways liberals use these destructive policies to their advantage?
3. How do you think the Government Accountability Pledge would help resolve these issues?

Chapter 13: Establishing Performance Measures

Our forefather's created this system of government so the individual states could pool their resources to help each other. It's a great concept and as we see throughout our nation's history, it works very well when allowed to work the way it was designed. However, during the Great Depression the way our government operated changed. Our nation went from a very limited federal government to a greatly expanded federal government looking to exert its power on the states. These changes resulted in unfunded mandates, increased taxation and a government largely unresponsive to the needs of the states and the citizens. These problems can all be traced back to an issue I identified in my first book, the lack of performance measures. As a contract between the citizens and the government, our Constitution is devoid of any method to provide quantifiable data on how our government is meeting its obligations.

The obligations are important since the

citizens would have no need for government if the obligations were not being fulfilled. A government failing to fulfill its obligations is doing nothing other than taking tax dollars and providing no benefit as a result. Our Founding Fathers had every intention of the government fulfilling the obligations set forth in the Constitution. Unfortunately, our government has come to be controlled by groups more concerned with their personal obligations than the obligations of the government. Our Founding Fathers did not create performance measures in the Constitution. They didn't feel the need for them because they did not foresee the day when the government would be so careless in the exercise of its powers or where the voters would become so lackadaisical in selecting individuals for public office.

The lack of performance measures in our Constitution has been magnified by the lack of performance measures in legislation requiring taxpayer funding. While policies devoid of performance measures can be frustrating, the use of these types of policies for taxation purposes is unethical. Only illegitimate governments pursue tax policies knowing there are no performance measures available. Once the government begins to tax citizens and businesses without any means of proving the effectiveness of the policy, there is little chance of rescinding the tax. Worse yet would be the government becoming dependant upon the taxes from the unethical policy. A classic example of this would, again, be the tax on tobacco products. The tax provides so much of the government's budget that it's now nearly impossible to actively stop the sale of tobacco products and make the nation healthier without doing serious economic harm.

One of the most noteworthy problems our nation is currently faced with where performance measures should be applied is in terms of environmental policies. There are some good environmental policies our government has passed. Policies which help provide for clean water and require companies to clean up accidents which have an impact on the environment. Recently, we have seen liberals pushing for more strict environmental policies which lack the performance measures necessary to scientifically prove the policy's effectiveness. Case in point would be the current movement towards "carbon credits". The lack of a stated sample error in the percentage of man made carbon in the earth's atmosphere means there is no way to prove the policy is having any impact at all[1]. To make matters even worse, scientists who present evidence to these facts are threatened and punished for telling the truth.

The lack of performance measures leaves the government unable to prove the impact of the law, be that a positive or negative impact. In essence, the government is throwing money at an issue with no means of knowing if the policy is achieving the desired goals. The inability to develop effective performance measures can be tied to any number of causes. In the worst case scenario, the policy does more harm than good, yet no one realizes the damage being done. Unfortunately, once the government begins collecting taxes and fees for the program it becomes almost impossible to end the program. Over time the program will be expanded to include more mandates without any performance measures. Eventually, the program will grow to the point of outliving its usefulness but because there is no proof of the failures, the program will continue draining money from the taxpayers.

There are a number of programs where we see the lack of performance measures impacting the government's ability to provide for the needs of the citizens. One in the news recently is the scandal within the Veterans Administration.[2] The failure of the government to provide performance measures to ensure patients are actually getting treatment resulted in a situation where administrators were under no pressure to ensure compliance with acceptable standards of care. Despite the obvious lack of accountability, the Obama Administration has yet to even suggest the implementation of performance measures as a means of combating the problem. The fact is, by implying the need for performance measures in this instance, the Obama Administration would have to concede that they failed to provide the appropriate performance measures for the Affordable Care Act. Here is a situation where one policy failure is creating another policy failure.

A similar situation is playing out currently in our nation's education system. The new Common Core standards are not performance based. Rather, the standard is based on the simple completion of a task without any emphasis on the work being done correctly. The goal of Common Core is to teach students the process for completing a task, not the right way to complete the task. No where in the Common Core "Myths and Facts" do they ever discuss the issue of performance[3]. This is similar to the mentality which resulted in the Veterans Administration fiasco. Doctors were required to treat a certain number of patients each day, but there was no standard on how they were to be treated. The Obama Administration is seeking to apply the same mentality, which has failed our nation's veterans, to the education of our nation's children. It doesn't take any magical powers to foretell the failure of the Common Core standards.

The primary reason our government lacks the performance measures necessary to ensure quality services and accountability is that liberals hate the idea of performance measures. The majority of policies championed by liberals would fail if basic performance measures were applied. Take for example gun control. For more than a decade, we have seen study after study which repeatedly confirms conceal carry laws reduce the rate of violent crime in communities. Furthermore, we see the cities with the strictest gun laws are also the cities with the highest homicide rates. Even the 1994 Assault Weapons Ban proved inefficient at preventing mass shootings, yet liberals champion the idea of a new ban every time a mass shooting occurs.[4] There is no performance measure which can be applied to show gun control works. This only goes to prove what conservatives have said all along, the goal of gun control is to deprive law abiding citizens of their rights. This highlights the need for performance measures to help protect the rights of individuals.

Without performance measures to provide quantifiable evidence of the effectiveness of a policy, the government is simply wasting money. This is not to say all effects of a policy are quantifiable, but the ones which are, provide substantial evidence which can be used to determine the validity of the policy's continued funding. The establishment of performance measures is an essential element of the Government Accountability Pledge. These performance measures would serve to not only hold the government accountable for the way it spends taxpayer money, but also provide evidence of how the government is functioning and provide an added safeguard for the rights of individual citizens.

Study Questions:

1. Can you think of a policy where performance measures would be useful?
2. Can you think of ways liberals use the lack of performance measure to their advantage?
3. How do you think performance measures would help restore the public's faith in government?

Chapter 14: Policies Must Solve a Problem

It should come as no surprise that taxes are part of living in the United States. Despite what some would like us to believe, taxes aren't bad. The government simply could not function without collecting taxes to pay for services. While no one likes to pay taxes, without taxes we would have no military, no roads, no schools, or any of the other necessities of a civilized society. The taxes are not the problem; the problem arises when the taxes are being generated by policies which fail to solve a problem. Worse yet is when the taxes do more harm than good for the citizens. This type of policy failure is an offshoot of the lack of performance measures. Policies which fail to solve a problem can actually have performance measures attached, creating the illusion of it being a good policy. As a result, the Government Accountability Pledge seeks to address these types of destructive policies before they become law.

One of the best examples of this type of policy is the Affordable Care Act. In creating this law, liberals looked to develop a means of requiring all citizens to have health insurance coverage[1]. Health insurance coverage is good and it helps to alleviate some of the financial burden of an unexpected illness or accident. We can even develop performance measures for the Affordable Care Act and look at the number of people who have health insurance now verses the number prior to the law going into effect. These are the exact performance measures being offered by the Obama Administration. However, since health insurance and access to care are not the real problems the United States is facing, these performance measures are useless in addressing health care reform.

Say you were driving your car and the transmission began to make a grinding sound. You take the car to a mechanic and you're told the air pressure in your tires is low. While the air pressure in your tires might be low, it has nothing to do with the grinding sound you hear from the transmission. The mechanic has provided you with a quantifiable issue with your car, but the information does nothing to reveal the cause of the original problem. This same situation is true of the current attempts at health care reform.

The United States does have a serious health care problem. In fact, it could be said our nation's health care system is terminally ill. The problem is not access to care, but too many people seeking care for health issues of their own creation. The health care system has become tremendously overburdened and as a result people have a difficult time getting in to see a doctor. In this case, supply and demand economics dictated an increase cost for medical care. As the cost went up, more people found they were unable to pay the rising cost and had to rely on government programs to receive health care. The end result was a government system which became burdened beyond its capacity.[2] The liberal answer to this problem was to address the symptom of the disease, to decrease the burden on the government programs liberals had created by forcing everyone to buy health insurance.

In looking at the nature of the problems facing our health care system, it becomes apparent where the actual trouble lies. The solution the Obama Administration offered for this problem not only failed to fix the problem, but made the problem much worse. It has actually become more difficult to get an appointment with a doctor because the system is more overburdened than before. With more individuals having insurance coverage, they are seeking medical treatment for issues they might not have had before. Furthermore, the cost of insurance premiums have increased so much that many individuals can no longer afford the cost of basic medical care[3]. This has resulted in an even heavier burden being placed on government health care programs. The Affordable Care Act is truly an example of a policy which not only failed to solve a problem, but actually made the problem worse.

Typically when we see policies which fail to solve a problem, it's because the individuals developing the policy failed to understand the nature of the problem. Going back to the car analogy used earlier, it's impossible for a mechanic to fix a car if the mechanic doesn't understand how the car works to begin with. Liberals have developed a different worldview based on ideas conceived by a long line of drug addicts. The notion of "third generation rights" is completely at odds with our form of government. The simple fact is, Liberals will never be able to fix the problems our society faces. No matter how well intentioned, they will never be able to solve the problems because of their worldview. We are a nation where the problems must ultimately be solved on an individual level and liberals will always look to solve problems by exerting control on the collective. The United States has never been successful in fixing a problem where the solution was applied at the societal level. None of the solutions liberals have offered for fixing our nation's problems have ever worked and the solutions never will. From the very beginning, our nation was founded on the concept of individuals freely working together for a greater good. The concept of individuality is at the core of the success the United States has enjoyed for so many years.

The proper solution for our nation's health care crisis would be methods designed to help each citizen live a healthier life. Unfortunately, this is not what the Affordable Care Act has established. Instead of developing solutions to the problem on an individual level, the Obama Administration looked to impose economic burdens which have little to no positive impact on the actual problem. The negative impacts of this failed attempt at health care reform are yet to be completely realized. What we do know is that the heavy burden of increased premiums will have a destructive effect on the U.S. economy[4]. The burden from the increased pressure from citizens requiring government assistance programs in combination with the tax subsidies will threaten the economic vitality of our nation. The Affordable Care Act was doomed to failure from the beginning because it failed to solve the true problems our nation faces.

The worst part is we as a nation know where this kind of policy ultimately leads. Over the last few decades we've seen this problem in the taxes levied on tobacco products. As medical science began to shed light on the health risks associated with tobacco use, the government began imposing higher taxes on those products with the intention of forcing the cost so high as to cause individuals to stop using the product. Ideally, the taxes should have been used in combination with performance measures to ensure the tax money collected was only used to treat individuals who developed medical conditions related to tobacco use. Under such a system the money collected from the tax would have decreased as tobacco use decreased and with the decrease in use, the need for medical care related to tobacco use would have decreased as well. The result would have been a tax only effecting tobacco users, and minimized any additional burden on the rest of the public. This is an example of how a tax should be used to address a specific problem. Ultimately, the tax would have fallen into disuse once tobacco use did as well.

Unfortunately, what has happened is the exact opposite; the taxes being generated by tobacco sales are going to fund schools, roads and other essentials the government provides. If the government were to either cease to tax tobacco products or ban the sale of tobacco products, the government would be in financial trouble. On the flip side, if the government does nothing, the use of tobacco will slowly bankrupt our nation in medical bills. As a nation, we're caught in a classic no win scenario. We can't afford to actually fight tobacco use and help citizens get healthy, but we also can't afford the mounting cost of medical care for the individuals who use tobacco products. The failure of the government to actually solve the problem has created an even bigger problem with no available solution.

The situation with taxing tobacco products provides a preview of what happens with all policies which fail to solve a problem. The policy always ends up, ultimately, doing more harm than good and causing the government to throw good money after bad. This is why voters must hold elected officials responsible for enacting policies which fail to solve a problem. The goal of including this in the Government Accountability Pledge is to prevent these policies from working their way into our government. Once a policy becomes law it can be incredibly difficult to get the law revoked. We are seeing this with attempts to revoke the Affordable Care Act. A massive amount of money has already been spent at both the state and federal levels to enact this policy. Revoking it now is the proper course of action for the financial security of the United States. However, it will cause layoffs in both the public and private sector. We're already in the no win scenario created by a policy which fails to solve the problem. The only solution to prevent these kinds of policies from being enacted in the future is to hold candidates accountable for supporting these policies.

Study Questions:

1. Can you think of a policy that failed to solve a problem?
2. Can you think of ways liberals use policy failures to their advantage?
3. What do you think ultimately happens when a policy fails to solve a problem?

Conclusion

Clearly the United States has some serious problems with which need to be dealt. Most of these problems are the result of failed policies. Unfortunately, many of these failed policies find their roots in the failed ideology of drug addiction we know as modern liberalism. It should come as no surprise that our government has taken on many of the characteristics of addiction. While lying to attack their political adversaries, liberals have spent the better part of the last century undermining the individual rights and values which were created to define the United States. The liberal drive to create policies which undermine the foundation our nation is built upon could lead nowhere but failure. From Wilson's 14 points and League of Nations, to Roosevelt's "New Deal", to Johnson's "Great Society" and most recently Obama's Affordable Care Act, liberals have forced one policy failure after another on the U.S. citizens.

The one piece of good news is this: we've seen enough of these bad policies that we can now identify them before they become law. By applying the guidelines laid out in the Government Accountability Pledge, our nation can not only begin to correct policy problems, but begin to heal our nation. Are liberals going to fight this? Absolutely! Liberals don't want our nation to succeed. The success of the United States is entirely dependant upon the success of the individual citizen. Liberals don't want you to develop, grow and succeed in developing as an individual. As President Obama said during his 2012 campaign:

> There are a lot of wealthy, successful Americans who agree with me—because they want to give something back. They know they didn't—look, if you've been successful, you didn't get there on your own. If you were successful, somebody along the line gave you some help. There was a great teacher somewhere in your life. Somebody helped to create this unbelievable American system that we have that allowed you to thrive. Somebody invested in roads and bridges. If you've got a business—you didn't build that. Somebody else made that happen.[1]

President Obama's words served as his endorsement of the progressive economic theory held by modern liberalism. He repeats the concept of "somebody" in regards to the idea that the government created and paid for services which helped the business owner to succeed. President Obama's words also reveal the liberals failure to realize "somebody" as an individual citizen who wanted our nation to succeed. "Somebody" is not a collective or a "sovereign state" declaring themselves ruler of the citizens as the worldview held by liberal ideology would suggest. Rather "somebody" was a citizen who woke up this morning and decided to contribute in a meaningful way to our nation. It is individual citizens, who pay their taxes, volunteer to fight in our military and cast votes, who allow the government to function. The United States didn't become a world power by riding the coat tails of others. We embraced individual responsibility and free will to develop a new form of government where all are equal in the eyes of the law. Now liberals want to trade God given equal rights for state sanctioned "third generation rights" which are anything but equal. I guess liberals can rationalize wasting tax dollars when it is "somebody" else's money.

I truly believe the tool required to get our nation back on course is the Government Accountability Pledge. We must begin by holding elected officials responsible for policies which are doomed to fail. Given enough time, a policy which begins by violating one of the four rules set out in the Government Accountability Pledge will eventually violate all four. Amnesty for illegal immigrants is a prefect example. As discussed in Chapter 12, the concept of amnesty violates the rule of law. It is unethical for the government to award criminals for breaking the law. If the government is going to reward those who break the law, then what reason would they have for respecting the law?

Previous amnesty programs have proven to do little to stop the flow of illegal immigrants. The simple fact is amnesty does not solve the problem. Previous amnesty programs resulted in more illegal immigrants flooding into the United States, hoping for amnesty to be declared again. Furthermore, amnesty did nothing to stop the practice of hiring illegal immigrants. The problem is illegal immigrants see an opportunity in the United States without the need to abide by our nation's laws. The liberal solution is to apply amnesty, knowing it won't work.

There is virtually no way to apply any meaningful performance measures to an amnesty program. Since illegal immigrants are not entering the U.S. through traditional border crossings and points of entry there is no way to account for an increase or decrease in numbers. Deportation numbers would prove useless since some of those being deported could have come here before the amnesty was declared and simply never applied for citizenship under the program. Our nation would have no means of determining the effectiveness of the program, yet we would still be spending billions on health care, schools and other government services for immigrants who benefited from this program.

Ultimately, liberals would seek to extend amnesty to illegal immigrants again. The same problems would still exist with the program and the program would still fail to solve the illegal immigration problem. How can U.S. citizens be expected to trust a government which keeps engaging in the same failed policy over and over again? If our government is faulty for acting this way, then we as citizens are just as much at fault if we allow the government to continue.

This is the path all bad policy takes and it will continue to do so until our elected officials begin to take responsibility for enacting good policies which are designed to avoid these pitfalls. Left unchecked, these types of destructive policies will destroy our nation. It's just a matter of time until the public coffers run dry. We can only kick the fiscal can down the road for so long and then we hit a dead end. It's the cumulative effect of multiple bad policies which has created the suicidal taxation spiral into which our nation is descending.

The Government Accountability Pledge is designed to curtail the destructive habits of liberals, and begin healing some of the damage which has been done over the pervious century. In corrections there is a saying: firm, fair, and consistent. This saying describes the manner in which offenders are dealt with, and I believe the same applies to liberals. Since the tactics liberals are utilizing are the same as those of a drug addict, it seems only appropriate to apply the same firm, fair and consistent standard to dealing with destructive liberal policies. The Government Accountability Pledge provides the necessary tool to be firm, fair and consistent in dealing with these destructive policies. At its most basic level, the Government Accountability Pledge represents the basic ideals which lead to transparent, responsive, and responsible government, and the citizens of the United States deserve nothing less. The rules within the pledge are just as applicable to conservative legislation as it is to liberal legislation. Any proposed bill which violates these rules should not be supported, regardless of which party is sponsoring it.

The level of distrust our citizens have in their government is unhealthy.[2] Our nation cannot continue on this path and be successful. I made the following statement in my first book and it bears repeating: "a government of the people, by the people and for the people" cannot exist without the trust of the people. Our nation must being to bridge the gap which has been created as a result of failed policies and the best way to accomplish this is to hold politicians accountable for the laws they pass. The Government Accountability Pledge provides the best tool I've found to achieve this goal and rebuild our nation.

Study Questions:

1. Can you think of a policy which would have benefited from the Government Accountability Pledge?
2. Can you think of reasons why some politicians would oppose the Government Accountability Pledge?
3. Would the Government Accountability Pledge begin to renew your faith in government?
4. Would you support a candidate who took the Government Accountability Pledge?

Post Script:
The Christian View of Modern Liberalism

As I did at the end of *Null and Void,* I want to provide some insight about the issues which have been discussed in this book with a focus on Christianity. Liberalism and Christianity hold two diametrically opposed worldviews. The simple fact is this, humanity is fatally flawed. Both liberals and conservatives know this to be true. The difference is how both sides deal with the flaw.

Liberals see every flaw the same, as a flaw of individuality to be dealt with in a communal context. In essence, the worldview of modern liberalism perceives the individual as flawed. This concept if derived from the theories developed by the liberal writers mentioned in Chapter One. Liberals, therefore, look to work together in social groups to overcome the flaw. According to liberal theory, the homogeny of the group covers up the perceived individual flaws and before long the flaws go unnoticed. When group think doesn't provide the solution to the personal problems and flaws, as is normally the case, the group members begin looking for other means of collectively dealing with the issue. One of the many ways liberals cope with this failure is through drug use. This is why we have a "drug culture" in our nation, because liberals are still looking for a social group to solve the problem, but being unable to find one they seek a social group to escape the problem.

Conservatives, many of whom are Christian, also perceive the flaw of humanity as an individual issue, but look to deal with the issue on an individual level. As Christians, we know this flaw as sin. We also understand the only solution for sin is to establish an individual relationship with Jesus Christ and thereby cleansing us of our sins in his redemptive blood. There is no social group which has the ability to deal with this problem for you. You can go to what ever church you want, you can listen to which ever evangelist you want, but at the end of the day the choice to accept Christ must be made by the individual.

This simple idea of how to deal with the sin nature of humanity is at the core of the difference between liberals and conservatives. Liberals look to take the same approach as Adam and Eve did in the Garden of Eden. Adam and Eve tried to hide from the problem, first by covering their nakedness and then by hiding from God when they became fearful of God's judgment for their transgression.[1] Liberals look to hide from sin by working in groups, taking drugs or other means of escape. By controlling what they believe to be individualism, liberals believe they can overcome this flaw in the human condition. This simply isn't true, but it doesn't stop them from trying. Inevitably, once liberals realize the error of their ways they look to hide from the problem again, creating a repetitive cycle.

This is not to say Christians never run from God. In fact, I feel pretty safe in saying every believer has run from God at some point. Even the Apostle Peter is said to have run from Rome when facing execution for his faith. The problem isn't necessarily running, but the willingness to turn back and follow despite the cost. In John 6:60-71 we see how many turned from Jesus and stopped following him because they determined the cost of discipleship to be too high.[2] In John 6:68-69 we see Peter's response to Jesus, the same response all Christians should have.[3] We know who Christ is and what he has done for us, so we have no other choice but to follow him as individuals.

God created us as individuals, to live as individuals and to come to repentance as individuals. Individuality at its most basic level is a gift from God. Without individuality we would be unable to accept Christ and seek forgiveness for our sins. To truly become an individual you must break from the sin nature and accept Christ. The act of accepting Christ is the first action of a true individual. Christ could lay down his life because it was an individual choice of a man free from the bondage of sin. Christ is providing us with the example of what it means to be individual. How can you expect to make other choices if you haven't accepted Christ first? The ability to make all other choices is predicated on being free to make the choice to begin with.

Individuality comes from reconnecting with God through the Holy Spirit. We see evidence of this in the Gospels. Throughout the four Gospels we see the apostles following Jesus and mimicking what he did or following with the social ideals of the day. An example of this can be found in John 11 when Jesus tells of Lazarus' death; Thomas quickly replies that the apostles should go with Jesus that they may die also[4]. This is seen again in Luke 22 when Jesus tells the apostles to prepare for what is to come and provides a list of items they will need.[5] This list is similar to the Armor of God as described in Ephesians 6.[6] However, when Jesus tells them to get a sword, meaning the word of God, the apostles respond by showing two actual swords. In both of these instances the disciples are simply saying what they believed Christ wanted to hear.

In Peter, we see the power of the Holy Spirit to transform a person into an individual. In Matthew 26 we read of Jesus predicting the denial of the apostles, and how Peter attempts to placate Jesus by insisting he won't deny Jesus.[7] Jesus knows Peter will fail and just hours later Peter is being cowered by an adolescent girl. Clearly, Peter isn't acting as an individual, but hiding from his failures and sin nature. However, something very different occurs in Acts 2 when the apostles are given over to the Holy Spirit.[8] The formerly mimicking, placating and cowardly Peter gives a powerful sermon as an individual, no longer fearful of sin or failure.

Freud claimed God was an illusion[9], and I don't mind someone questioning the existence of God. However, I will never understand why anyone would turn to the words of drug addicts when seeking to answer questions about God. In reality it's sin which creates the illusion of individuality in the mind of the unrepentant. Sin will cause a person to create ideas in their mind to justify not accepting salvation. A perfect example of this is the person who feels they have done something "too bad" to be forgiven. It is also the illusion of individuality which has the ability to create problems for us when applied improperly. The improper application of what is perceived as individuality creates a prideful person unwilling to repent. God is omnipotent and as a result only a prideful person would stand in opposition to God. This is seen in liberalism, which arrogantly proclaims the state to be sovereign in place of God. Where liberals act as guilty prisoners unwilling to acknowledge their sins and seek forgiveness, conservative Christians accept our sin nature and rejoice in the pardon we have received.

God has dealt with the prideful before. We're told of how Satan was forced from God's heavenly kingdom due to his prideful ways. It should come as no surprise for liberals to demonstrate the same prideful mentality which resulted in Satan's banishment. Liberalism has taken to not only discouraging true individuality through the acceptance of Christ, but liberals are actually seeking to embrace the prideful mindset of the sinner. We see this most clearly in the "gay pride" movement. Liberals insist homosexuality cannot be a sin because of all the people who are involved in the culture. From the liberal mindset, this collective of people cannot be in sin since the illusionary individual is flawed but the collective is perfect. The problem is, even in their collective state, they are still exhibiting the illusion of individual traits. The very notion of pride is the most powerful aspect of this illusion and therefore subject to sin.

For liberalism, homosexuality is simply a means of attacking Christianity. The far left has no use for homosexuals other than to pursue the liberal agenda. To the liberal elite, homosexuals represent a fringe minority which they will deal with when the time is right. Christianity poses a much larger threat to modern liberalism and the liberal desire to destroy individuality. Homosexuality presents a perfect tool for liberals to use for this purpose. Liberals have taken to Christ's commandment in John 13:31-35, that we as disciples should love one another[10], and they are corrupting it to mean homosexuality is acceptable. Nothing could be further from the truth of what Christ taught. When Jesus spoke of love he was not referring to love in a sexual context. Homosexuality, and any other sinful sexual act, is an act of prideful selfishness. This is not to say sex is bad. God created sex for a purpose, and misusing it for selfish purposes is wrong. When Jesus taught to love one another he meant in humbleness and selflessness. Jesus wanted his disciples to love our fellow humans as he loved us, all the way to the cross.

This does not mean believers should hate homosexuals or any other sinner. Christ calls his followers to love sinners the same way God loved us since the foundation of the world. I personally find myself praying harder for sinners than for those who have accepted Christ and have been saved. I don't want to see any soul lost, but I also know there are groups in the world who are determined to prevent people from achieving their individuality and gaining salvation. To this end many liberals have taken to twisting the words of Christ to shame Christians into abandoning their faith.

This is most evident in the liberal claim of Matthew 7:1 "Judge not, that ye be not judged.[11]" The far left has taken this to mean declaring an act sinful is judging someone else. In modern times we use the word "judge" to mean making a decision about something another person is doing. People tell others to stop "judging them", or ask why someone is "being so judgmental". The concept of a person having the ability to judge others is based in modern psychology. However, in 1 A.D., the word judge was used in a purely legal sense. When a judgment was handed down by the pro consuls, kings, or emperor, it was a verdict. In modern vernacular the more appropriate word to use in place of "judge" would be "condemn", thus the reason when the Matthew 7:1 passage is repeated in Luke 6:37, the passage also reads "condemn not, lest ye be condemned.[12]" The ideas of judgment and condemnation are connected. Once the judge arrives at a verdict or judgment, then the sentence condemns the person to their punishment.

The true condemnation comes when we refuse to take efforts to turn someone from the ways of sin. If you know a person is living a sinful life and you do nothing to help them seek redemption, then you are in essence acknowledging the person being deserving of destruction. If they died at that very moment without repenting, then you believe the sins this person has committed makes them worthy of the destruction of their eternal soul. The important word here is "acknowledge", meaning as a believer you know the result. We know from Romans 6:23 that the end result of any sin without repentance is death[13]. In James 5:19-20 we are taught "Brethren, if any of you do err from the truth, and one convert him; Let him know, that he which converteth the sinner from the error of his way shall save a soul from death, and shall hide a multitude of sins.[14]" We are all sinners, whether we are redeemed, unredeemed or unrepentant, and God sent his son to die for all sinners. This can be little worse than a believer who accepts God's free gift of salvation, only to make attempts to deny the same to other sinners. Yet this is exactly what many liberals want to do. It's the spiritual equivalent of a doctor failing to tell a patient he or she has a serious medical problem needing treatment.

Liberals and conservatives alike understand our nation has this disease, yet liberals refuse to acknowledge the treatment required. Liberals keep insisting our nation was not founded on Christian principles. These same liberals don't understand the individual nature of our nation. True individuality and Christianity go hand in hand. It is impossible to truly express individuality when in bondage to sin. Our nation would not exist as it does today without a strong Christian foundation. If we continue to allow the degradation of the presence of Christian beliefs in our nation, our nation has no hope of continuing. Without a Christian foundation and the related concept of individuality, a nation governed by the will of individual citizens cannot exist. It is imperative that the conservative movement take action to preserve the Christian foundation which has helped our nation to prosper since its inception.

Notes

Chapter 1

[1] Fabian, G. (2013) Karl Marx Prince of Darkness. Bloomington, IN: Xlibris. pp. 11
[2] Fabian, G. (2013) Karl Marx Prince of Darkness. Bloomington, IN: Xlibris. pp. 11
[3] Nietzsche, F. (1990) Beyond Good and Evil. New York: Penguin. pp. 44
[4] Nietzsche, F. (1977) The Portable Nietzsche. (W. Kaufmann Trans.) New York: Penguin. pp. 93
[5] Nietzsche, F. (1883) "Letter to Peter Gast August 1883". (Online). Available:http://en.wikisource.org/wiki/Selected_Letters_of_Friedrich_Nietzsche#To_Peter_Gast_-_August.2C_1883
[6] Cate, C. (2005) Friedrich Nietzsche. New York: Overlook Press. pp. 389, 453
[7] Strachey, J (1990) The Ego and the Id (The Standard Edition of the Complete Psychological Works of Sigmund Freud). New York: Norton.
[8] Freud, S. (2006) Interpreting Dreams. (J.A. Underwood Trans.) New York: Penguin.
[9] Strachey, J (1989) The Future of Illusion (The Standard Edition of the Complete Psychological Works of Sigmund Freud). New York: Norton.
[10] Jones, E. (1953) Sigmund Freud: Life and Work, vol. 1. London: Hogarth Press. pp 94-97.
[11] Freud, S. (1985) The Complete Letters of Sigmund Freud to Wilhelm Fliess, 1887-1904. (J. Masson, Trans.) Cambridge, Harvard University Press. pp. 49, 106, 127

Chapter 2

[1] Baldor, L.C. (2014, June 1) Hagel: Captive's Life was in Danger. Associated Press Online, [Online] Available: http://bigstory.ap.org/article/hagel-captives-life-was-danger

[2] Cassata, D. (2014, June 7) Bergdahl Swap a Flashpoint of Rival Charges. Associated Press Online, [Online] Available: http://bigstory.ap.org/article/bergdahl-swap-flashpoint-rival-charges.

[3] Dilanian, K. and Riechmann, D. (2014, June 3) Questions Loom over Bergdahl-Taliban Swap. Associated Press Online, [Online] Available: http://bigstory.ap.org/article/us-soldier-released-after-5-years-captivity.

[4] Baldor, L. C. and Klapper, B. (2014, June 11) In Hill Testimony, Hagel Defends Bergdahl Trade. Associated Press Online, [Online] Available: http://bigstory.ap.org/article/hagel-testifies-wednesday-taliban-prisoner-swap

[5] Jaconi, M. (Executive Producer), Baktar, R. (Director) (2014, June 8). State of the Union. Cable News Network. Transcript Available: http://transcripts.cnn.com/TRANSCRIPTS/1406/08/sotu.02.html.

[6] Weisman, J. and Savage, C. (2012, June 28) House Finds Holder in Contempt Over Inquiry on Guns. The New York Times, [Online] Available: http://www.nytimes.com/2012/06/29/us/politics/fast-and-furious-holder contempt-citation-battle.html?pagewanted=all&_r=0

[7] United States Department of Commerce, National Oceanic and Atmospheric Administration. (2014). Trends in Atmospheric Carbon Dioxide. Washington D.C. [Online] Available:http://www.esrl.noaa.gov/gmd/ccgg/trends/global.html

[8] Lott, J. (2010) More Guns, Less Crime: Understanding Crime and Gun Control Laws (3rd ed.) Chicago: University of Chicago Press.

Chapter 3

[1] Sutter, J.D. (2012, June 19) Google Reports 'Alarming' Rise in Government Censorship Requests. Cable NewsNetwork. [Online] Available:http://www.cnn.com/2012/06/18/tech/web/google-transparency-report/

[2] Tooley, M. D. (2006, Feburary 9) The "God Hates Fags" Left. Front Page Magazine. [Online] Available: http://archive.frontpagemag.com/readArticle.aspx?ARTID=5606

[3] Lott, J. (2010) More Guns, Less Crime: Understanding Crime and Gun Control Laws (3rd ed.) Chicago: University of Chicago Press.

Chapter 4

[1] United States Department of Health and Human Services, Health Resources and Services Administration. (2014). Hill-Burton Free and Reduced-Cost Health Care. Washington D.C. [Online] Available:http://www.hrsa.gov/gethealthcare/affordable/hillburton/.

[2] Gorman, A. (2014, August 26) Transgender Woman Feels 'Complete" Thanks to Obamacare. Cable News Network. [Online] Available: http://www.cnn.com/2014/08/26/health/obamacare-transgender-surgery/

[3] McCarthy, A. C. (2014, February 20) Obama's 'Blame It on The Video' Was a Fraud for Cairo as Well as Benghazi — More Proof. National Reveiw. [Online] Available:http://www.nationalreview.com/corner/371565/obamas-blame-it-video-was-fraud-cairo-well-benghazi-more-proof-andrew-c-mccarthy.

[4] Waterman, S. (2013, May 13) Benghazi Scapegoat Remains in Prison for Film. Washinton Times. [Online] Available: http://www.washingtontimes.com/news/2013/may/13/benghazi-scapegoat-filmmaker-remains-prison/

Chapter 5

[1] Simon, L.H. (Ed.). (1994). Karl Marx: Selected Writings. Indianapolis, IN: Hackett Publishing. pp. 186.

[2] Kelly, M. (1993, May 13) Political Memo; Re-examining the Fine Print On Clinton's Tax Promises. The New York Times. [Online] Available: http://www.nytimes.com/1993/01/26/us/political-memo-re-examining-the-fine-print-on-clinton-s-tax-promises.html

[3] United States Congress. (1993). H.R.2264 -- Omnibus Budget Reconciliation Act of 1993. 103rd Congress. Washington D.C. United States Government Printing Office.

[4] United States Small Business Administration. (2010). The Impact of Regulatory Costs on Small Firms. Washington D.C. [Online] Available: http://www.sba.gov/advocacy/impact-regulatory-costs-small-firms.

[5] Gramm, P. and Solon, M. (2013, August 12). The Clinton-Era Roots of the Financial Crisis. Wall Street Journal. [Online] Available: http://online.wsj.com/news/articles/SB10001424127 887323477604579000571334113350

[6] O'Toole, J. (2014, June 24). Meet the Marxist Behind Seattle's Wage Hike. Cable News Network. [Online] Available: http://money.cnn.com/2014/06/24/news /economy/seattle-marxist-minimum-wage/.

Chapter 6

[1] Maraniss, D. (1998, January 28) First Lady Launches Counterattack. Washington Post, p. A1 [Online] Available: http://www.washingtonpost.com/wp-srv/politics/special/clinton/stories/hillary012898.htm.

[2] McCarthy, A. C. (2014, February 20) Obama's 'Blame It on The Video' Was a Fraud for Cairo as Well as Benghazi — More Proof. National Reveiw. [Online] Available:http://www.nationalreview.com/corner/371565/ obamas-blame-it-video-was-fraud-cairo-well-benghazi-more-proof-andrew-c-mccarthy.

[3]Sherfinski, D. (2014, May 15) Issa subpoenas Kerry to testify on Benghazi; SecState so far 'unavailable'. The Washington Times, [Online] Available: http://www.washingtonpost.com/wpsrv/politics/special/clinton /stories/hillary012898.htm.

[4] Slater, A. (2012, August 10) Voter ID laws: the Republican ruse to disenfranchise 5 million Americans. The Guardian, [Online] Available: http://www.theguardian.com/ commentisfree/2012/aug/10/voter-id-laws-republican ruse-disenfranchise

[5] Kutler, S. (2014, April 4) The Republican 'Great White Hope:' Manipulating Election Laws. Huffington Post, [Online] Available: http://www.huffingtonpost.com/stanley-kutler/the-republican-voter-id-laws_b_5086369.html.

[6] Ellsberg, D. (2002). Secrets: A Memoir of Vietnam and the Pentagon Papers. New York: Viking. pp. 9-10.

[7] Greenwald, G. (2013, June 6). NSA collecting phone records of millions of Verizon customers daily. The Guardian. [Online] Available: http://www.theguardian.com/world /2013/jun/06/nsa-phone-records-verizon-court-order.

[8] Shear, M. D. and Weisman, J. (2013, May 13). Obama Dismisses Benghazi Furor but Assails I.R.S. The New York Times. [Online] Available: http://www.nytimes.com/2013/05/14/us/politics/obama-addresses-benghazi-and-irs-controversies.html?_r=0

[9] Bade, R. (2014, May 7). Republicans hit IRS' Lois Lerner with contempt. Politico.com. [Online] Available: http://www.politico.com/story/2014/05/lois-lerner-irs-contempt-of-congress-106464.html

Chapter 7

[1] Darwin, C. Appleman, P. (Ed.) (2002) The Origin of Species. New York: Norton. (Original work published 1859).

[2] McKee, J. K., Poirier, F. E., and McGraw, W.S. (2005) Understanding Human Evolution (5th ed.) Upper Saddle River, NJ: Pearson Education. pp. 6-7.

[3] Holy Bible: King James Version. (1987). The First Epistle of Paul the Apostle to the Corinthians. Nashville, TN: Thomas Nelson. pp. 546.

[4] United Nations. (1948, December 9). Convention on the Prevention and Punishment of the Crime of Genocide. Paris [Online] Available: http://www.un.org/ga/search /view_doc.asp?symbol=a/res/260(III).

[5] United States Government. White House. (2013, September 10). Remarks by the President in Address to the Nation on Syria. Washington D.C. [Online] Available http://www.whitehouse.gov/the-press office/2013/09/10/remarks-president-address-nation-syria

[6] United States Government. White House. (2013, September 10). Remarks by the President in Address to the Nation on Syria. Washington D.C. [Online] Available http://www.whitehouse.gov/the-press office/2013/09/10/remarks-president-address-nation-syria

[7] United States Government. White House. (2013, January 16). Remarks by the President and Vice President on Gun Violence. Washington D.C. [Online] Available http://www.whitehouse.gov/the-press office/2013/01/16/remarks-president-and-vice-president-gun-violence.

[8] United States Government. White House. (2009, October 5). Executive Order 13514 - - Focused on Federal Leadership in Environmental, Energy and Economic Performance. Washington D.C. [Online] Available: http://www.whitehouse.gov/the-press-office/president-obama-signs-executive-order-focused-federal-leadership environmental-ener.

[9] Londoño, E. and Miller, G. (2013, September 11). CIA begins weapons delivery to Syrian rebels. The Washington Post [Online] Available: http://www.washingtonpost.com/world/national-security /cia-begins-weapons-delivery-to-syrian-rebels/2013/09/11/9fcf2ed8-1b0c-11e3-a628-7e6dde8f889d_story.html.

[10] Ibrahim, R. (2013, November 26). Largest Massacre of Christians in Syria Ignored. Christian Post. [Online] Available: http://www.christianpost.com/news/largest-massacre-of-christians-in-syria-ignored-109566/.

[11] Human Rights Watch (2013, November 19). Syria Opposition Abuses During Ground Offensive hrw.org. [Online] Available: http://www.hrw.org/news/2013/11/19/ syria-opposition-abuses-during-ground-offensive.

[12] Chulov, M. (2013, August 15). Egypt's Coptic Christians report fresh attacks on churches. The Guardian [Online] Available: http://www.theguardian.com/world/2013 /aug/15/egypt-coptic-christians-attacks-churches.

Chapter 8

[1] Cameron, I. (Executive Producer). (2013, May 19)This Week with George Stephanopoulos. American Broadcasting Company. New York: [Online] Transcript: http://abcnews.go.com/Politics/week-transcript-white house-senior-adviser-dan-pfeiffer/story?id=19204852 #.UZ6UaqI-Zm0

[2] Schmidt, M. S. (2013, February 20). Jesse Jackson Jr. Pleads Guilty in Campaign Money Case. The New York Times. [Online] Available: http://www.nytimes.com/2013/02 /21/us/politics/jesse-l-jackson-jr-pleads-guilty-to wire-and-mail-fraud.html

[3] Cook, D. (2009, April 13). Former Representative William Jefferson Sentenced to 13 years in Prison. Christian Science Monitor. [Online] Available: http://www.csmonitor.com/USA/Politics/2009/1113/former-rep-william-jefferson-sentenced-to-13-years-in-prison

[4] Savage, C. (2011, March 21). Attack Renews Debate Over Congressional Consent. The New York Times [Online] Available: http://www.nytimes.com/2011/03/22/world/ Africa/22powers.html

[5] United States Department of Justice. (2010, July 16). Memorandum for the Attorney General (Re: Applicability of Federal Criminal Laws and the Constitution to Contemplated Lethal Operations Against Shaykh Anwar al Aulaqi). Washington D.C. [Online] Available: http://www.foxnews.com/politics/interactive/2014/ 06/23/memo-on-targeted-killing-al-awlaki/ pp. 16

[6] United States Congress. (1994). H.R.3355.EAH – Violent Crime Control and Law Enforcement Act of 1994. 103rd Congress. Washington D.C. United States Government Printing Office.

[7] United States Library of Congress. (1994). H.R.3355.EAH – Violent Crime Control and Law Enforcement Act of 1994. 103rd Congress. Washington D.C. United States Government Printing Office. [Online] Available: http://thomas.loc.gov/cgi-bin/bdquery/z?d103:HR03355:@@@X

[8] United States Library of Congress. (1994). H.R.3355.EAH – Violent Crime Control and Law Enforcement Act of 1994. 103rd Congress. Washington D.C. United States Government Printing Office. [Online] Available: http://thomas.loc.gov/cgi-bin/bdquery/z?d103:HR03355:@@@X

[9] United States Government. White House. (2013, January 16). Remarks by the President and Vice President on Gun Violence. Washington D.C. [Online] Available http://www.whitehouse.gov/the-press office/2013/01/16/remarks-president-and-vice-president-gun-violence.

[10] United States Supreme Court. 554 U.S. 570 (2008, June 26). District of Columbia et al v. Heller (No 07-290). Washington D.C. United States Government Printing Office. [Online] Available: http://www.supremecourt.gov/opinions/boundvolumes/554bv.pdf

[11] United States Supreme Court. 573 U.S. ___ (2014, June 26). National Labor Relations Board v. Noel Canning et al (No 12-1281). Washington D.C. United States Government Printing Office. [Online] Available: http://www.supremecourt.gov/opinions/13pdf/12-1281_mc8p.pdf

[12]Holy Bible: King James Version. (1987). The Gospel According to Matthew. Nashville, TN: Thomas Nelson. pp. 470.

Chapter 9

[1] Riddell, K. (2014, May 18). 'High Risk' label from feds puts gun sellers in banks' crosshairs, hurts business. The Washington Times [Online] Available: http://www.washingtontimes.com/news/2014/may/18/targeted-gun-sellers-say-high-risk-label-from-feds/?page=alll

[2] Yeomans, W. The tea party's terrorist tactics. Politico [Online] Available:http://www.politico.com/news/stories /0711/60202.html

[3] McKinnon, J.D. and Hughes, S. Wider Problems Found at IRS. The Wall Street Jounral [Online] Available: http://online.wsj.com/news/articles/SB10001424127887324715704578478851998004528?mg=reno64wsj&url=http%3A%2F%2Fonline.wsj.com%2Farticle%2FSB10001424127887324715704578478851998004528.html

[4] Cable News Network. E-mails: Ex-IRS official Lois Lerner queried Sen. Chuck Grassley invitation. Cable News Network [Online] Available: http://www.cnn.com/2014/06/25/politics/irs-lois-lerner-chuck-grassley-email/

[5] Fields, L. (2013, December 7). Judge Orders Colorado Bakery to Cater for Same-Sex Weddings. American Broadcasting Corporation [Online] Available: http://abcnews.go.com/US/judge-orders-colorado-bakery-cater-sex-weddings/story?id=21136505

[6] Lincoln, A. (1863, November 19) Gettysburg Address.

[7] Harrington, E. (2014, August 26) Feds creating database to track hate speech on Twitter. Fox News. [Online]. Available: http://www.foxnews.com/politics/2014/08/26/feds-creating-database-to-track-hate-speech-on-twitter/

[8] United States Department of Defense. Operation Desert Fox. Website. [Online] Available: http://www.defense.gov/specials/desert_fox/

[9] Hitchens, C. (1999). No One Left To Lie To: The Triangulations of William Jefferson Clinton. New York: Verso.

[10] Ellsberg, D. (2002). Secrets: A Memoir of Vietnam and the Pentagon Papers. New York: Viking. pp. 9-10.

[11] Gustin, G. (2009, August 9) Protestors rally at closed union office. St. Louis Post-Dispatch. p. A4.

[12] Newcomb, A. (2011, November 3). Sexual Assaults Reported in 'Occupy' Camps. American Broadcasting Corporation. [Online] Available: http://abcnews.go.com/US/sexual-assaults-occupy-wall-street-camps/story?id=14873014

Chapter 10

[1] Ernst, D. (2014, July 11). Violent gang taking advantage of immigration crisis, using border as recruiting hub. The Washington Times. [Online]. Available: http://www.washingtontimes.com/news/2014/jul/11/violent-gang-ms-13-taking-advantage-immigration-cr/

[2] Seper, J. (2013, June 5). U.S. sanctions top members of MS-13 gang. The Washington Times. [Online]. Available: http://www.washingtontimes.com/news/2013/jun/5/treasury-department-sanctions-top-members-ms-13/

[3] Gehrke, J. (2014, July 24). Nancy Pelosi on Border: 'Use This Crisis' to Pass Immigration Reform. The National Review. [Online]. Available: http://www.nationalreview .com/corner/383639/nancy-pelosi-border-use-crisis-pass immigration-reform-joel-gehrke

[4] Nietzsche, F. (1990) Beyond Good and Evil. New York: Penguin. pp. 44

[5] Levin Institute. Negative vs. Positive Rights. State University of New York. [Online] Available: http://www.globalization101.org/negative-vs-positive-rights/

[6] United Nations. (1992, June 14). Rio Declaration on Environment and Development. Rio de Janeiro [Online] Available: http://www.un.org/documents/ga/conf151 /aconf15126-1annex1.htm

[7] United Nations. (1992, June 14). Rio Declaration on Environment and Development. Rio de Janeiro [Online] Available: http://www.un.org/documents/ga/conf151 /aconf15126-1annex1.htm

[8] Nietzsche, F. (1977) The Portable Nietzsche. (W. Kaufmann Trans.) New York: Penguin. pp. 93

[9] Jefferson, T. (1776) The Declaration of Independence. Philadelphia.

[10] United States Congress. (1830, May 26) Indian Removal Act. 21st Congress, 1st Session. Washington D.C.: United States Government Printing Office. [Online] Available: http://www.loc.gov/rr/program/bib/ourdocs /Indian.html

[11] Henretta, J., Brody, D., Ware, S. and Johnson, M. S. (2000) America's History (4th ed., Vol. 1) Boston, MA. St. Martin. pp. 420-429.
[12] Henretta, J., Brody, D., Ware, S. and Johnson, M. S. (2000) America's History (4th ed., Vol. 1) Boston, MA. St. Martin. pp. 441-443.
[13] United States Congress. (1866, April 9) Civil Rights Act of 1866. 39th Congress, 1st Session. Washington D.C.: United States Government Printing Office.
[14] United States Congress. (1870, May 30) Enforcement Act of 1870. 44th Congress, 2nd Session. Washington D.C.: United States Government Printing Office.
[15] Wolgemuth, K. L. (1959). Woodrow Wilson and Federal Segregation. The Journal of Negro History. Vol. 44 Num. 2: pp. 158–173.
[16] Gerstle, G. and Cooper J. M., (ed.) Reconsidering Woodrow Wilson: Progressivism, Internationalism, War, and Peace. Washington D.C.: Woodrow Wilson International Center For Scholars. pp 103-104.
[17] Gerstle, G. and Cooper J. M., (ed.) Reconsidering Woodrow Wilson: Progressivism, Internationalism, War, and Peace. Washington D.C.: Woodrow Wilson International Center For Scholars. pp 103-104.
[18] Grady, D. (2007, January 23). White Doctors, Black Subjects: Abuse Disguised as Research. The New York Times. [Online]. Available: http://www.nytimes.com/2007/01/23/health/23book.html
[19] Davis,A. (1981) Women, Race and Class. New York: Random House. pp. 203
[20] Congressional Research Service. (2010, February 26). American War and Military Operations Casualties: List and Statistics. Washington D.C.: United States Government Printing Office_[Online] Available: http://fas.org/sgp/crs/natsec/RL32492.pdf
[21] Congressional Research Service. (2010, February 26). American War and Military Operations Casualties: List and Statistics. Washington D.C.: United States Government Printing Office_[Online] Available: http://fas.org/sgp/crs/natsec/RL32492.pdf

Chapter 11

[1] United Nations. (1992, June 14). Rio Declaration on Environment and Development. Rio de Janeiro [Online] Available: http://www.un.org/documents/ga/conf151/aconf15126-1annex1.htm

[2] Greenwald, G. (2013, June 6). NSA collecting phone records of millions of Verizon customers daily. The Guardian. [Online] Available: http://www.theguardian.com/world/2013/jun/06/nsa-phone-records-verizon-court-order.

[3] United Nations. (1992, June 14). Rio Declaration on Environment and Development. Rio de Janeiro [Online] Available: http://www.un.org/documents/ga/conf151/aconf15126-1annex1.htm

Chapter 12

[1] Cameron, I. (Executive Producer). (2013, May 19)This Week with George Stephanopoulos. American Broadcasting Company. New York: [Online] Transcript: http://abcnews.go.com/Politics/week-transcript-white house-senior-adviser-dan-pfeiffer/story?id=19204852#.UZ6UaqI-Zm0

[2] Cameron, I. (Executive Producer). (2013, May 19)This Week with George Stephanopoulos. American Broadcasting Company. New York: [Online] Transcript: http://abcnews.go.com/Politics/week-transcript-white house-senior-adviser-dan-pfeiffer/story?id=19204852#.UZ6UaqI-Zm0

[3] United States Supreme Court. 573 U.S. ___ (2014, June 26). National Labor Relations Board v. Noel Canning et al (No 12-1281). Washington D.C. United States Government Printing Office. [Online] Available: http://www.supremecourt.gov/opinions/13pdf/12-1281_mc8p.pdf

Chapter 13

[1] United States Department of Commerce, National Oceanic and Atmospheric Administration. (2014). Trends in Atmospheric Carbon Dioxide. Washington D.C. [Online] Available: http://www.esrl.noaa.gov/gmd/ccgg /trends/global.html

[2] Bronstein, S. and Griffin, D. (2014, April 23) A fatal wait: Veterans languish and die on a VA hospital's secret list. Cable News Network. [Online] Available: http://www.cnn. com/2014/04/23/health/veterans-dying-health-care-delays/

[3] Common Core State Standard Initiative. Myths vs. Facts. Common Core State Standard Initiative. [Online]. Available: http://www.corestandards.org/about-the-standards/myths-vs-facts/

[4] Lott, J. (2010) More Guns, Less Crime: Understanding Crime and Gun Control Laws (3rd ed.) Chicago: University of Chicago Press.

Chapter 14

[1] United States Congress. (2010, March 23) Public Law 11-148 – Patient Protection and Affordable Care Act. 111th Congress, 2nd Session. Washington D.C.: United States Government Printing Office.

[2]United States Department of Health and Human Services. (2008 September) The Effect of Health Care Cost Growth on the U.S. Economy. Washington D.C. [Online] Available:http://aspe.hhs.gov/health/reports/08/ healthcarecost/report.html

[3] Gottlieb, S. (2014, May 15). First Obamacare Premium Notices For 2015 Show Double Digit Increases. Forbes. [Online]. Available: http://www.forbes.com/sites/ scottgottlieb/2014/05/15/first-obamacare-premium-notices-for 2015-show-double-digit-increases/

[4] Harrison, J.D. (2014, February 25) Obama administration: Health law's new rules will increase costs for most small businesses. The Washington Post. [Online]. Available: http://www.washingtonpost.com/business/on-small business/obama-administration-health-laws-new-rules-will-increase-costs-for-most-small businesses/2014/02/24/0623d01e-9d9c-11e3-9ba6-800d1192d08b_story.html

Conclusion

[1] Obama, B. (2012, July 13). Roanoke, VA Campaign Speech. Available: http://www.c-span.org/video/?307056 2/president-obama-campaign-rally-roanoke

[2] Mataconis, D. (2014, August 8). Public trust in government hits new lows. Christian Science Monitor. [Online]. Available: http://www.csmonitor.com/USA/DC-Decoder/Decoder-Voices/2014/0808/Public-trust-In-Government-hits-new-lows

Post Script

[1] Holy Bible: King James Version. (1987). Book of Genesis. Nashville, TN: Thomas Nelson. pp. 2.

[2] Holy Bible: King James Version. (1987). The Gospel According to John. Nashville, TN: Thomas Nelson. pp. 510.

[3] Holy Bible: King James Version. (1987). The Gospel According to John. Nashville, TN: Thomas Nelson. pp. 510.

[4] Holy Bible: King James Version. (1987). The Gospel According to John. Nashville, TN: Thomas Nelson. pp. 513.

[5] Holy Bible: King James Version. (1987). The Gospel According to Luke. Nashville, TN: Thomas Nelson. pp. 502 503.

[6] Holy Bible: King James Version. (1987). The Epistle of Paul the Apostle to the Ephesians. Nashville, TN: Thomas Nelson. pp. 562.

[7] Holy Bible: King James Version. (1987). The Gospel According to Matthew. Nashville, TN: Thomas Nelson. pp. 472.

[8] Holy Bible: King James Version. (1987). The Acts of the Apostles. Nashville, TN: Thomas Nelson. pp. 520-521.

[9] Strachey, J (1989) The Future of Illusion (The Standard Edition of the Complete Psychological Works of Sigmund Freud). New York: Norton.

[10] Holy Bible: King James Version. (1987). The Gospel According to John. Nashville, TN: Thomas Nelson. pp. 515.

[11] Holy Bible: King James Version. (1987). The Gospel According to Matthew. Nashville, TN: Thomas Nelson. pp. 460.

[12] Holy Bible: King James Version. (1987). The Gospel According to Luke. Nashville, TN: Thomas Nelson. pp. 491.

[13] Holy Bible: King James Version. (1987). The Epistle of Paul the Apostle to the Romans. Nashville, TN: Thomas Nelson. pp. 541.

[14] Holy Bible: King James Version. (1987). The Epistle of James. Nashville, TN: Thomas Nelson. pp. 580.

Sources Cited

Bade, R. (2014, May 7). Republicans hit IRS' Lois Lerner with contempt. Politico.com. [Online] Available: http://www.politico.com/story/2014/05/lois-lerner-irs-contempt-of-congress-106464.html

Baldor, L.C. (2014, June 1) Hagel: Captive's Life was in Danger. Associated Press Online, [Online] Available: http://bigstory.ap.org/article/hagel-captives-life-was-danger

Baldor, L. C. and Klapper, B. (2014, June 11) In Hill Testimony, Hagel Defends Bergdahl Trade. Associated Press Online, [Online] Available: http://bigstory.ap.org/article/hagel-testifies-wednesday-taliban-prisoner-swap

Bronstein, S. and Griffin, D. (2014, April 23) A fatal wait: Veterans languish and die on a VA hospital's secret list. Cable News Network. [Online] Available: http://www.cnn.com/2014/04/23/health/veterans-dying-health-care-delays/

Cable News Network. E-mails: Ex-IRS official Lois Lerner queried Sen. Chuck Grassley invitation. Cable News Network [Online] Available: http://www.cnn.com/2014 /06/25/politics/irs-lois-lerner-chuck-grassley-email/

Cameron, I. (Executive Producer). (2013, May 19)This Week with George Stephanopoulos. American Broadcasting Company. New York: [Online] Transcript: http://abcnews.go. com/Politics/week-transcript-white-house-senior-adviser-dan-pfeiffer/story?id=19204852#.UZ6UaqI-Zm0

Cassata, D. (2014, June 7) Bergdahl Swap a Flashpoint of Rival Charges. Associated Press Online, [Online] Available: http://bigstory.ap.org/article/bergdahl-swap-flashpoint-rival-charges

Cate, C. (2005) Friedrich Nietzsche. New York: Overlook Press.

Chulov, M. (2013, August 15). Egypt's Coptic Christians report fresh attacks on churches. The Guardian [Online] Available: http://www.theguardian.com/world/2013/aug/15/egypt-coptic-christians-attacks-churches

Common Core State Standard Initiative. Myths vs. Facts. Common Core State Standard Initiative. [Online]. Available: http://www.corestandards.org/about-the-standards/myths-vs-facts/

Congressional Research Service. (2010, February 26). American War and Military Operations Casualties: List and Statistics. Washington D.C.: United States Government Printing Office [Online] Available: http://fas.org/sgp/crs/natsec/RL32492.pdf

Cook, D. (2009, April 13). Former Representative William Jefferson Sentenced to 13 years in Prison. Christian Science Monitor. [Online] Available: http://www.csmonitor.com/USA/Politics/2009/1113/former-rep-williamjefferson-sentenced-to-13-years-in-prison

Darwin, C. Appleman, P. (Ed.) (2002) The Origin of Species. New York: Norton. (Original work published 1859).

Davis,A. (1981) Women, Race and Class. New York: Random House.

Dilanian, K. and Riechmann, D. (2014, June 3) Questions Loom over Bergdahl-Taliban Swap. Associated Press Online, [Online] Available: http://bigstory.ap.org/article/us-soldier-released-after-5-years-captivity

Ellsberg, D. (2002). Secrets: A Memoir of Vietnam and the Pentagon Papers. New York: Viking.

Ernst, D. (2014, July 11). Violent gang taking advantage of immigration crisis, using border as recruiting hub. The Washington Times. [Online]. Available: http://www.washingtontimes.com/news/2014/jul/11/violent-gang-ms-13 taking-advantage-immigration-cr/

Fabian, G. (2013) Karl Marx Prince of Darkness. Bloomington, IN: Xlibris.

Fields, L. (2013, December 7). Judge Orders Colorado Bakery to Cater for Same-Sex Weddings. American Broadcasting Corporation [Online] Available: http://abcnews.go.com/US/judge-orders-colorado-bakery-cater-sex-weddings/story?id=21136505

Freud, S. (1985) The Complete Letters of Sigmund Freud to Wilhelm Fliess, 1887-1904. (J. Masson, Trans.) Cambridge, Harvard University Press.

Freud, S. (2006) Interpreting Dreams. (J.A. Underwood Trans.) New York: Penguin.

Gehrke, J. (2014, July 24). Nancy Pelosi on Border: 'Use This Crisis' to Pass Immigration Reform. The National Review. [Online]. Available: http://www.nationalreview.com/corner/383639/nancy-pelosi-border-use-crisis-pass-immigration-reform-joel-gehrke

Gerstle, G. and Cooper J. M., (ed.) Reconsidering Woodrow Wilson: Progressivism, Internationalism, War, and Peace. Washington D.C.: Woodrow Wilson International Center For Scholars.

Gorman, A. (2014, August 26) Transgender Woman Feels 'Complete" Thanks to Obamacare. Cable News Network. [Online] Available: http://www.cnn.com/2014/08/26/health/obamacare-transgender-surgery/

Gottlieb, S. (2014, May 15). First Obamacare Premium Notices For 2015 Show Double Digit Increases. Forbes. [Online]. Available: http://www.forbes.com/sites/scottgottlieb/ 2014/05/15/first-obamacare-premium-notices-for 2015-show-double-digit-increases/

Gramm, P. and Solon, M. (2013, August 12). The Clinton-Era Roots of the Financial Crisis. Wall Street Journal. [Online] Available: http://online.wsj.com/news/articles/SB10001 424127887323477604579000571334113350

Grady, D. (2007, January 23). White Doctors, Black Subjects: Abuse Disguised as Research. The New York Times. [Online]. Available: http://www.nytimes.com/2007/01 /23/health/23book.html

Greenwald, G. (2013, June 6). NSA collecting phone records of millions of Verizon customers daily. The Guardian. [Online] Available: http://www.theguardian.com/world/2013/jun/ 06/nsa-phone-records-verizon-court order

Gustin, G. (2009, August 9) Protestors rally at closed union office. St. Louis Post-Dispatch. p. A4.

Harrington, E. (2014, August 26) Feds creating database to track hate speech on Twitter. Fox News. [Online]. Available: http://www.foxnews.com/politics/2014/08/26/feds-creating-database-to-track-hate-speech-on-twitter/

Harrison, J.D. (2014, February 25) Obama administration: Health law's new rules will increase costs for most small businesses. The Washington Post. [Online]. Available: http://www.washingtonpost.com/business/on-small business/obama-administration-health-laws-new-rules-will-increase-costs-for-most-small businesses/2014/02/24/0623d01e-9d9c-11e3-9ba6-800d1192d08b_story.html

Henretta, J., Brody, D., Ware, S. and Johnson, M. S. (2000) America's History (4th ed., Vol. 1) Boston, MA. St. Martin.

Hitchens, C. (1999). No One Left To Lie To: The Triangulations of William Jefferson Clinton. New York: Verso.

Holy Bible: King James Version. (1987). Nashville, TN: Thomas Nelson.

Human Rights Watch (2013, November 19). Syria Opposition Abuses During Ground Offensive hrw.org. [Online] Available: http://www.hrw.org/news/2013/11/19/syria-opposition-abuses-during-ground-offensive

Ibrahim, R. (2013, November 26). Largest Massacre of Christians in Syria Ignored. Christian Post. [Online] Available: http://www.christianpost.com/news/largest-massacre-of-christians-in-syria-ignored-109566/

Jaconi, M. (Executive Producer), Baktar, R. (Director) (2014, June 8). State of the Union. Cable News Network. Transcript Available: http://transcripts.cnn.com/TRANSCRIPTS/1406/08/sotu.02.html

Jefferson, T. (1776) The Declaration of Independence. Philadelphia.

Jones, E. (1953) Sigmund Freud: Life and Work, vol. 1. London: Hogarth Press.

Kelly, M. (1993, May 13) Political Memo; Re-examining the Fine Print On Clinton's Tax Promises. The New York Times. [Online] Available: http://www.nytimes.com /1993/01/26/us/political-memo-re-examining-the-fine print-on-clinton-s-tax-promises.html

Kutler, S. (2014, April 4) The Republican 'Great White Hope:' Manipulating Election Laws. Huffington Post, [Online] Available: http://www.huffingtonpost.com /stanley-kutler/the-republican-voter-id-laws_b_5086369.html

Levin Institute. Negative vs. Positive Rights. State University of New York. [Online] Available: http://www. globalization101.org/negative-vs-positive-rights/

Lincoln, A. (1863, November 19) Gettysburg Address.

Londoño, E. and Miller, G. (2013, September 11). CIA begins weapons delivery to Syrian rebels. The Washington Post [Online] Available: http://www.washingtonpost.com /world/national-security/cia-begins-weapons-delivery-to -syrian-rebels/2013/09/11/9fcf2ed8-1b0c-11e3-a628-7e6dde8f889d_story.html

Lott, J. (2010) More Guns, Less Crime: Understanding Crime and Gun Control Laws (3rd ed.) Chicago: University of Chicago Press.

Maraniss, D. (1998, January 28) First Lady Launches Counterattack. Washington Post, p. A1 [Online] Available: http://www.washingtonpost.com/wp-srv/politics/ special/clinton/stories/hillary012898.htm

Mataconis, D. (2014, August 8). Public trust in government hits new lows. Christian Science Monitor. [Online]. Available: http://www.csmonitor.com/USA/DC-Decoder/Decoder-Voices/2014/0808/Public-trust-In-government-hits-new-lows

McCarthy, A. C. (2014, February 20) Obama's 'Blame It on The Video' Was a Fraud for Cairo as Well as Benghazi — More Proof. National Reveiw. [Online] Available: http://www.nationalreview.com/corner/371565/obamas-blame-it-video-was-fraud-cairo-well-benghazi-more-proof-andrew-c-mccarthy

McKee, J. K., Poirier, F. E., and McGraw, W.S. (2005) Understanding Human Evolution (5th ed.) Upper Saddle River, NJ: Pearson Education.

McKinnon, J.D. and Hughes, S. Wider Problems Found at IRS. The Wall Street Jounral [Online] Available: http://online.wsj.com/news/articles/SB10001424127887324715704578478851998004528?mg=reno64 wsj&url=http%3ª%2F%2Fonline.wsj.com%2Farticle%2FSB10001424127887324715704578478851998004528.html

Newcomb, A. (2011, November 3). Sexual Assaults Reported in 'Occupy' Camps. American Broadcasting Corporation. [Online] Available: http://abcnews.go.com/US/sexual-assaults-occupy-wall-street-camps/story?id=14873014

Nietzsche, F. (1990) Beyond Good and Evil. New York: Penguin.

Nietzsche, F. (1883) "Letter to Peter Gast August 1883". (Online). Available:http://en.wikisource.org/wiki/Selected_Letters_of_Friedrich_Nietzsche#To_Peter_Gast_-_August.2C_1883

Nietzsche, F. (1977) The Portable Nietzsche. (W. Kaufmann Trans.) New York: Penguin.

Obama, B. (2012, July 13). Roanoke, VA Campaign Speech. Available: http://www.c-span.org/video/?307056 2/president-obama-campaign-rally-roanoke

O'Toole, J. (2014, June 24). Meet the Marxist Behind Seattle's Wage Hike. Cable News Network. [Online] Available: http://money.cnn.com/2014/06/24/news/economy/seattle-marxist-minimum-wage/

Riddell, K. (2014, May 18). 'High Risk' label from feds puts gun sellers in banks' crosshairs, hurts business. The Washington Times [Online] Available: http://www.washingtontimes.com/news/2014/may/18/targeted-gun-sellers say-high-risk-label-from-feds/?page=all

Savage, C. (2011, March 21). Attack Renews Debate Over Congressional Consent. The New York Times [Online] Available: http://www.nytimes.com/2011/03/22/world/Africa/22powers.html

Schmidt, M. S. (2013, February 20). Jesse Jackson Jr. Pleads Guilty in Campaign Money Case. The New York Times. [Online] Available:http://www.nytimes.com/2013/02/21/us/politics/jesse-l-jackson-jr-pleads-guilty-to-wire-and-mail-fraud.html

Seper, J. (2013, June 5). U.S. sanctions top members of MS-13 gang. The Washington Times. [Online]. Available: http://www.washingtontimes.com/news/2013/jun/5/treasury-department-sanctions-top-members-ms-13/

Simon, L.H. (Ed.). (1994). Karl Marx: Selected Writings. Indianapolis, IN: Hackett Publishing.

Shear, M. D. and Weisman, J. (2013, May 13). Obama Dismisses Benghazi Furor but Assails I.R.S. The New York Times. [Online] Available: http://www.nytimes.com/2013/05/14/us/politics/obama-addresses-benghazi-and-irs controversies.html?_r=0

Sherfinski, D. (2014, May 15) Issa subpoenas Kerry to testify on Benghazi; SecState so far 'unavailable'. The Washington Times, [Online] Available: http://www.washingtonpost.com/wpsrv/politics/special/clinton/stories/hillary012898.htm

Slater, A. (2012, August 10) Voter ID laws: the Republican ruse to disenfranchise 5 million Americans. The Guardian, [Online] Available: http://www.theguardian.com/commentisfree/2012/aug/10/voter-id-laws-republican ruse-disenfranchise

Strachey, J (1989) The Future of Illusion (The Standard Edition of the Complete Psychological Works of Sigmund Freud). New York: Norton.

Sutter, J.D. (2012, June 19) Google Reports 'Alarming' Rise in Government Censorship Requests. Cable News Network. [Online] Available: http://www.cnn.com/2012/06/18/tech/web/google-transparency-report/

Tooley, M. D. (2006, Feburary 9) The "God Hates Fags" Left. Front Page Magazine. [Online] Available: http://archive.frontpagemag.com/readArticle.aspx?ARTID=5606

United Nations. (1948, December 9). Convention on the Prevention and Punishment of the Crime of Genocide. Paris [Online] Available: http://www.un.org/ga/search/view_doc.asp?symbol=a/res/260(III)

United Nations. (1992, June 14). Rio Declaration on Environment and Development. Rio de Janeiro [Online] Available: http://www.un.org/documents/ga/conf151/aconf15126-1annex1.htm

United States Congress. (1830, May 26) Indian Removal Act. 21st Congress, 1st Session. Washington D.C.: United States Government Printing Office. [Online] Available: http://www.loc.gov/rr/program/bib/ourdocs/Indian.html

United States Congress. (1866, April 9) Civil Rights Act of 1866. 39th Congress, 1st Session. Washington D.C.: United States Government Printing Office.

United States Congress. (1870, May 30) Enforcement Act of 1870. 44th Congress, 2nd Session. Washington D.C.: United States Government Printing Office.

United States Congress. (1993). H.R.2264 -- Omnibus Budget Reconciliation Act of 1993. 103rd Congress. Washington D.C. United States Government Printing Office.

United States Congress. (1994). H.R.3355.EAH – Violent Crime Control and Law Enforcement Act of 1994. 103rd Congress. Washington D.C. United States Government Printing Office.

United States Congress. (2010, March 23) Public Law 11-148 – Patient Protection and Affordable Care Act. 111th Congress, 2nd Session. Washington D.C.: United States Government Printing Office.

United States Department of Commerce, National Oceanic and Atmospheric Administration. (2014). Trends in Atmospheric Carbon Dioxide. Washington D.C. [Online] Available: http://www.esrl.noaa.gov/gmd/ccgg /trends/global.html

United States Department of Defense. Operation Desert Fox. Website. [Online] Available: http://www.defense.gov/ specials/desert_fox/

United States Department of Health and Human Services. (2008 September) The Effect of Health Care Cost Growth on the U.S. Economy. Washington D.C. [Online] Available: http://aspe.hhs.gov/health/reports/08/healthcarecost /report.html

United States Department of Health and Human Services, Health Resources and Services Administration. (2014). Hill-Burton Free and Reduced-Cost Health Care. Washington D.C. [Online] Available:http://www.hrsa.gov/gethealthcare /affordable/hillburton/

United States Department of Justice. (2010, July 16). Memorandum for the Attorney General (Re: Applicability of Federal Criminal Laws and the Constitution to Contemplated Lethal Operations Against Shaykh Anwar al Aulaqi). Washington D.C. [Online] Available: http://www.foxnews.com/politics/interactive/2014/06/23/memo-on targeted-killing-al-awlaki/

United States Government. White House. (2009, October 5). Executive Order 13514 - - Focused on Federal Leadership in Environmental, Energy and Economic Performance. Washington D.C. [Online] Available: http://www.whitehouse.gov/the-press-office/president-obama-signs-executive-order-focused-federal-leadership environmental-ener

United States Government. White House. (2013, January 16). Remarks by the President and Vice President on Gun Violence. Washington D.C. [Online] Available http://www.whitehouse.gov/the-press-office/2013 /01/16/remarks-president-and-vice-president-gun-violence

United States Government. White House. (2013, September 10). Remarks by the President in Address to the Nation on Syria. Washington D.C. [Online] Available: http://www.whitehouse.gov/the-press-office/2013/09/10/remarks-president-address-nation-syria

United States Library of Congress. (1994). H.R.3355.EAH – Violent Crime Control and Law Enforcement Act of 1994. 103rd Congress. Washington D.C. United States Government Printing Office. [Online] Available: http://thomas.loc.gov/cgibin/bdquery/z?d103: HR03355:@@@X

United States Small Business Administration. (2010). The Impact of Regulatory Costs on Small Firms. Washington D.C. [Online] Available: http://www.sba.gov /advocacy/impact-regulatory-costs-small-firms

United States Supreme Court. 554 U.S. 570 (2008, June 26). District of Columbia et al v. Heller (No 07-290). Washington D.C. United States Government Printing Office. [Online] Available: http://www.supremecourt.gov/opinions /boundvolumes/554bv.pdf

United States Supreme Court. 573 U.S. ___ (2014, June 26). National Labor Relations Board v. Noel Canning et al (No 12-1281). Washington D.C. United States Government Printing Office. [Online] Available: http://www.supremecourt.gov/opinions/13pdf/12-1281_mc8p.pdf

Waterman, S. (2013, May 13) Benghazi Scapegoat Remains in Prison for Film. Washinton Times. [Online] Available: http://www.washingtontimes.com/news/2013/may/13/ benghazi-scapegoat-filmmaker-remains-prison/

Weisman, J. and Savage, C. (2012, June 28) House Finds Holder in Contempt Over Inquiry on Guns. The New York Times, [Online] Available: http://www.nytimes.com /2012/06/29/us/politics/fast-and-furious-holder contempt-citation-battle.html?pagewanted=all&_r=0

Wolgemuth, K. L. (1959). Woodrow Wilson and Federal Segregation. The Journal of Negro History. Vol. 44 Num. 2.

Yeomans, W. The tea party's terrorist tactics. Politico [Online] Available: http://www.politico.com/news/stories/0711/60202. html

www.ingramcontent.com/pod-product-compliance
Lightning Source LLC
Chambersburg PA
CBHW060301290526
45789CB00001B/372
* 9 7 8 1 5 0 0 6 8 2 6 3 7 *